NAVY
DIVERS

NAVY DIVERS

GREGOR SALMON

EBURY
PRESS

An Ebury Press book
Published by Random House Australia Pty Ltd
Level 3, 100 Pacific Highway, North Sydney NSW 2060
www.randomhouse.com.au

First published by Ebury Press in 2011

Addresses for companies within the Random House Group can be found at
www.randomhouse.com.au/offices

National Library of Australia
Cataloguing-in-Publication Entry

Salmon, Gregor.
Navy divers/Gregor Salmon.

ISBN 978 1 74166 657 1 (pbk.)

Australia. Royal Australian Navy. Clearance Diving Branch.
Divers – Australia.
Navies – Australia – Amphibious operations.

359.9840994

Cover design by Blue Cork
Front cover photo of Matthew Johnson, Clearance Diving Team 4, and back cover photo by LSIS
Phil Cullinan/RAN
Internal design and typesetting by Post Pre-Press Group
Printed in Australia by Griffin Press, an accredited ISO AS/NZS 14001:2004 Environmental
Management System printer

CONTENTS

ONE
GATES OF HELL

TWO DAYS INTO 'hell week', recruit Number 4 collapsed. He had just about run himself to death, his faculties so impaired you'd have thought he'd spent all night on the turps. Indeed, the medics treating him resembled cops overriding the will of a belligerent drunk. They stated things he didn't want to hear and he argued back, wielding his fists for emphasis. 'You're off course,' they told him several times, firmly and plainly. These death-knell words struck deeply into Number 4's addled brain, sounding a desperate alarm. He'd run hundreds of kilometres to prepare for this diver selection course. And, generally speaking, he'd known full well what to expect – ten days, maybe twelve, of torture – and he was ready. Beyond fit, he was so highly conditioned as to be physically *over*-qualified. He could run all day. He could do 120 sit-ups, sixty push-ups and eighteen palms-out chin-ups – twice the entry benchmarks – without hardly breaking a sweat. Lining up with nineteen other hopefuls to begin the gruelling trial, he didn't expect to just pass; he expected to shine. Some star recruit: spat out like pie gristle on day *two*. It was like he had no business being there in the first place.

Those windbags down at HMAS *Cerberus*, the navy's main training base in Western Port, Victoria, were right after all. For all the time he'd been camped down there waiting and training – the better part of a year had passed before he finally got to front diver selection – there were older sailors from the fleet, his fitness trainers, who would talk him down. They told him he wouldn't make the cut; he didn't have the goods. The jibes were mostly harmless attempts at a reality check, but sometimes Number 4 sensed there was envy at work. He felt they'd have been pleased if he'd given up on being a diver then and there. To some fleet boys, the divers were a bit uppity, a bunch of sunbaking fitness freaks who couldn't handle a boat bigger than a Zodiac. They saw themselves as a force apart, deriding regular navy for its watch-keeping and painting-and-decorating chores at sea. Divers thought they were a little bit special – and perhaps deep down the fleet sailors knew there was some truth to the boast. Perhaps they weren't sure whether they themselves had the right stuff to pass. And if *they* didn't, who was this young wannabe to believe that *he* did? Regardless, just on stats alone, it was an almost even-money bet that Number 4 would end up being just another diver reject, wringing his mind for clues as to what to do with his life next.

'Choose your rate, choose your fate', was a common retort from would-be divers, rubbing in the fact that they could earn more, see more and do more than regular sailors – if they made it, that is. *You don't know what I'm capable of,* was Number 4's silent comeback whenever his prospects were questioned. *What the hell do you know of my character?* Before he joined the navy at twenty-two, Number 4 was running a steady plumbing business with his brother. Off the clock he was a promising endurance athlete aiming to represent Australia, probably in kayaking. He wasn't devoted to one sport in particular; a new event would pique his interest and he would set about trying to win it. He would train like a demon before work, turn up to the job site at seven, finish at four and then train again. He always felt knackered but it was a lifestyle he enjoyed. Then something came along and seized his imagination like nothing before: clearance diving.

Out of the blue a paratrooper mate told Number 4 that he should make a career change, and that clearance diving was the answer. What on earth was clearance diving? It sounded like some strange fringe sport, like underwater hockey. But after listening to his friend and viewing all the online videos he could find, Number 4 grew convinced that he'd found his calling. He imagined action-packed times ahead, leading a life that was half trade, half adventure: diving every day; training every day; doing underwater repairs on ships with hydraulic chainsaws, drills, rivet guns and welders; conducting covert operations, demolitions and bomb disposals.

Five months later he was an enlisted seaman, billeted down at *Cerberus*. For a year he kept fit and did all the courses the navy required of him, itching for diver selection to roll around. When that day finally arrived, he packed his bags for HMAS *Penguin*, the home of the Royal Australian Navy Diving School at Balmoral on Sydney's Middle Head. At last, he was going to learn to be a clearance diver. He just had to pass the screen test.

≈

The Clearance Diver Acceptance Test, or CDAT (*see-dat*) for short, is more geared towards rejection than acceptance. It's the door bitch you must get past to enter the clearance diving world, and she has a piercing eye for weakness. CDAT is a chain of various high-intensity activities and challenges relieved by brief, irregular and altogether insufficient spells of rest. Other than the legendary Cadre Course – the SAS's formidable door bitch – CDAT is the most exacting selection trial in the Australian armed services. The new candidates don't know much about CDAT before they begin because divers don't share many details, mostly because they are hard-pressed to remember them. Such vagueness sustains CDAT's air of mystery. Whatever a recruit manages to glean, he would have taken to heart one ominous fact: diver selection is a physical and psychological ordeal bordering on torture. It has to be. They're not picking spin-class instructors here; they're selecting guys who can be counted on to render a skittish mine safe, while they're alone, under water, and staring into zero visibility. It's not everyone's cup of tea.

CDAT has to dig deeper than physicality and personality. Its aim is to unearth a fundamental character trait: the right stuff. There are no in-between grades, no coaching and no backslaps. You either pass or fail, and do so purely on how you perform and conduct yourself. Participation is absolutely voluntary so, as soon as you decide you don't want to be there anymore, you just raise your hand and you're gone. You can't walk in off the street. You must enlist, complete your seamanship course, basic dive course, psych and aptitude tests, and then wait. If your application to attempt CDAT is accepted, you are sent a list of items to bring, consisting mostly of PT gear – a heads-up that you are in for a flogging. It's a rare recruit who is not the least bit spooked by the CDAT mystique, and that's just the way the diving school likes it.

On arrival, you lose your name and you get a number. It's emblazoned in reflective silver on the back and front of the flouro vest you must wear every waking minute while on course. That's all the trainers need to identify, assess and address you.

By way of welcome, the trainers led Number 4 and his peers out the gates of *Penguin* and over to the old sergeants' mess at Chowder Bay. The 'gate-to-gate' is the traditional gut-busting opener to the course, a gruelling four-hour session designed to expose as many pretenders as possible. There are sprints along the way, and more sprints up forty-five-degree inclines, and more sprints up hundreds of steps, and an untold number of bodyweight exercises. This was the door bitch getting straight down to business, sorting the weak from the strong. When the exhausted recruits finally reached *Penguin*, they were told that they'd just completed the warm-up and were heading straight back out to do it all over again. Four recruits quit then and there.

Right from the outset motivation is put under the torch. If you don't have something solid to grab onto, something that sustains your purpose no matter what the pain, then you will find yourself in trouble very quickly. That something has to be more concrete than God and more genuine than ego. It has to be something real and personal – a hard-won habit, a promise, a loved one, a cause – that will inspire you to hold firm when all your weaknesses have been exposed and left flapping in the breeze. You need to have it in you – whatever 'it' is – to never give in.

Those who hung on were smashed by day's end. They hit the sack asking themselves, *What the fuck am I doing here?* At the same time, they were stoked: they'd been pushed beyond their limits and they'd survived. God knows what they'd be put through next, but even getting to that stage – a bed on the first night – was a win. And each candidate could take strength from knowing that everyone else was struggling too.

The next morning's PT session was a run from Manly back to *Penguin*, a distance of around eighteen kilometres. The route followed a coastal bush track that traced the northern shoreline of Sydney Harbour. Number 4 figured that this session – or 'evolution' – was right up his alley.

Naturally, he couldn't help but tackle it with a competitive mindset. Also, he was just plain eager to stand out. So he made a race of it.

The day was warming its way towards becoming Sydney's second hottest for the year. It was Melbourne Cup day. While the recruits gathered at Manly and set off on their run, other men their age boarded ferries for the city, took seats in the sun and looked forward to clocking off for the classic horse-race and getting on the piss. Number 4 had only one race in mind, and it was all in his head. He went out hard.

Running, however, was just one part of the session. The route they followed was beaded with several parks and stretches of open land. At each spot, the trainers gathered the recruits together and made them do squat-holds, sprints, sit-ups, push-ups and whatever else they saw fit to impose. Then it was fill your water bottles and off. All up, the run took three and a half hours.

It was mid-morning when Number 4 approached the finish line at Balmoral Beach, the south end of which adjoins *Penguin* base. The temperature was nearing 37°C and the humidity was high. Suddenly, a hundred metres out, his legs started to give way. He slowed down, began to stagger and then fell. Other candidates rushed in to catch him. They sat him down and called for help.

Arriving in seconds, the medics asked Number 4 questions to test whether he was correctly orientated to time, place and person. On that front he seemed okay: he knew who he was, where he was and what he was doing. But his mind was not okay; it was AWOL. The young recruit was encephalopathic.

His brain was so oxygen-deprived it was tripping. As the medics pressed ice packs all over his body and hooked him up to an intravenous drip, Number 4 started with the crazy talk. He thought he was in a pub. He said the reason he was so out of it was because someone had spiked his water bottle. He said he'd drunk a couple of beers, as though explaining why he was acting drunk. He then declared that there was beer in his water bottle, and he tipped the contents out to show them.

Confusion was understandable given Number 4's dehydration and high body temperature, but the loopy babble was a worry. For the medics, it was a cut-and-dried case of extreme heat exhaustion – there was no way he was going to be able to continue on with CDAT. They told him he was off course. He didn't take it well and lashed out. 'No, I'm not,' he insisted repeatedly. They brought in a doctor from the Submarine and Underwater Medicine Unit, the medical facility based at the dive school. He agreed: Number 4 was definitely off. Again, Number 4 refused to accept the decision – he'd come good, for sure.

That's what they all say: *I want to get back out there.* It's what they're expected to say. They pretend that their will is unbroken when it's shattered. But the medics can see the truth in their eyes. Yet for all Number 4's nonsense, there was no countermand whatsoever to be found there.

Once the medics had moved Number 4 to the treatment area, they told him to lie down. He refused. Another exhausted candidate was brought in and put on a drip. He was told to lie down and did so. Somehow Number 4 knew that any slim hope he had of pulling himself out of this nightmare would be lost if he did the same. Yet another recruit appeared. Although four years older than Number 4, he had a similar profile: an endurance athlete whose competitiveness had got the better of him. In his downtime, Number 20 liked to compete in 240 kilometre ultra-marathons through the Sahara Desert at the rate of a marathon a day. After a couple of hours on the drip the doctor told Number 20 he was good to get back on course. By that, the doctor meant for him to wait for the next car to Chowder Bay, where the rest of the recruits were paddling Zodiacs for a couple of hours before dismantling them and lugging them back to the dive school. The next thing the doctor knew, Number 20 had vanished. He'd just donned his runners and bolted over to join the others.

As the drip rehydrated Number 4's blood, his senses returned. He helped the saturation process along by drinking from his water bottle constantly. Feeling more clear-headed, he started thinking about what failure meant. Instead of progressing to the next stage, the basic clearance diving course where the diver apprenticeship really began, he was going to join the long line of cast-offs: one of those guys who prided himself on being in top nick, who lapped up the dark myths surrounding the navy's most elite branch and had daydreamed himself into the role, buying a commando watch the size of a hockey puck. This was the type of misguided egoist who CDAT, with its ruthless hunt for flaws, would make short work of, and Number 4's Achilles heel had been found all too easily.

He only had himself to blame. No one said the Manly run was a race. It was just the next evolution you had to get yourself through. All recruits were in the same boat. Having been hammered the previous day in hot weather, each had started behind the eight ball. Their bodies had not fully rehydrated and a scorcher of a day was building. Most had the sense to pace themselves. This was a day for the 'grey men' – the guys who are never first and never last, who don't stand out but are there at the end, where it counts. Blitzing the course meant nothing, but blowing out was a serious error of judgement. No one gave a damn about Number 4 collapsing and being put off course. He was just another nameless casualty. Obviously, he didn't have the right stuff.

Number 4 imagined delivering the news to his parents and girlfriend. How could he go back, look them in the eye and confess that he'd failed? He wouldn't be able to tell anyone anything about CDAT, he'd wiped out so quickly. The scenarios floating around in his head sickened him, but he remained determined to stop them from becoming reality. He actually had the audacity to believe that all was not lost. He drank and drank, and kept on at the medics, urging them to reassess him.

Number 4 was treated for four hours. During that time, six litres of fluid were put into him via the drip. In time, the medics relented and tested his urine to see how well his kidneys were working. That Number 4 was hydrated enough to urinate was a surprise in itself. As for his results, they were all pretty much normal – 'normal' being the state of physiological stress you'd expect to see in the other recruits. There was no denying it: Number 4 had recovered. The speed of his rebound had the medics stunned. They'd seen so many fit young men crash and burn on CDAT, and they'd seen plenty recover as well, but Number 4's turnaround was extraordinary. Here he was, sitting up, demanding to be put back into the game. Eventually, they had no medical reason to hold him back. The doctor agreed, but Number 4 needed to be set straight. If he ended up off his face on a covert mission, he could get men killed. If he was allowed back on course, the doctor said, Number 4 would have to prove to the medics that he could manage himself better. One more crash and he was gone. Number 4 said he understood, and with that he was released.

Later that day the medics got the results of Number 4's initial blood test. The evidence showed his body had been in a dire state. Under the extreme heat, exercise and dehydration, his brain had commenced on a radical course to ensure its own, and hence the body's, survival. It had begun shifting blood away from the most dispensable body parts, like the kidneys, to where it was desperately needed, like the brain itself, the heart, and the quad muscles Number 4 was relying on to run. But Number 4's kidneys had been copping it on two fronts. Because his body had run out of sugar, it had begun breaking down his skeletal muscles to get fuel. This is the early stage of rhabdomyolysis, or muscle meltdown. As a result, large proteins had entered his bloodstream and were blocking his kidneys. Thanks to the medics, Number 4 did not end up in hospital. But it was sheer will that saved him.

Five hours after being on the brink of renal failure, Number 4 was running back into hell.

≈

By day six there were thirteen recruits left and they'd been moved to Pittwater Annex, the dive school's second home. The base is lodged on the shore of the vast recreational harbour that shadows Sydney's northern-most beaches. Built in 1941, the Annex was originally a torpedo testing facility where weapons were finetuned before being issued to submarines. The navy needed to make sure that every self-propelled missile could fly straight and long enough to hit a designated target. The missiles were loaded onto a railcar in the main boatshed and wheeled out along a wharf-side track to the firing shed. Once fired, the torpedo would fly out, crash into the water and zoom up Pittwater for five kilometres or so. Adjustments were made, if necessary, before the torpedo was fitted with a warhead and carried into theatre. In the end, Pittwater wasn't big enough for both torpedoes and leisure craft, so the range was closed. The firing shed was pulled down in 1983 and the dive school had the place to themselves.

Removing the shed enhanced an already regal view of what Governor Phillip had described as 'the finest piece of water I ever saw'. Looking out from the base, a broad fairway of water extends north to the horizon, hemmed in by rugged hills to the west and the Barrenjoey Peninsula to the east. The scene is a postcard cliché: yachts tugging lazily at their moorings, sails dotting the open water, sticky-beak gulls on wharf pylons. At the far end lies a divot of land called Lion Island, standing vigil at the mouth of the Hawkesbury River. At night you can see the outcrop's lonely red beacon, while just to its right and a few kilometres beyond the candescent Ettalong beckons like the lamp of an inn. To the CDAT recruits this vista was little more than a peripheral blur. Riding out hell week, they were in no mood to stop and smell the roses. They hadn't been introduced to the local environment so much as fed to it. To them, Pittwater wasn't a fine stretch of water; it was an interminably long swimming pool in which they found themselves, day and night, finning for hours on end. West Head wasn't a magnificent national park; it was a heartbreaking bush gym, an outdoor stress lab fitted out with steep tracks, stairs, rope climbs and long, empty roads. Palm Beach wasn't a perfect little getaway; it was a heinous tract of leg-draining, energy-sucking sand that stuck to your wet clothes and glassed your skin raw. Pittwater was a willing accomplice in their breaking down.

Inside the boatshed, the recruits would emerge from their dorms and shuffle here and there over floorboards and rusty rail tracks at double time. Their faces were expressionless, their eyes fixed only a metre ahead. They appeared to be staring inward, as though trying their hardest not to forget an item of great importance. They were locked on single tasks. They told themselves over and over, *Just round this next bend and then you can relax.* To dwell on the hundred more ungodly hours to go was madness. The only optimism was to be found in fractions.

By this time it was hard enough for the recruits to stand up and stay awake. Their sleep-starved brains were running on faint wattage. On average they'd had about three hours of sleep a night, and there was hardly any downtime between tasks. When they weren't being flogged they were scoffing down their meals or washing their clothes or keeping the boatshed in good order. Riding from point A to point B by boat or bus to the next evolution gave them the odd chance to power nap. Most would go to sleep immediately. Others would just stare ahead, dozing with their eyes open. A good night's slumber was a sublime fantasy with a dark edge: the freedom to enjoy that luxury next could just as well come from failing the course as finishing it. Whenever they did get to their bunks they would fall asleep as if by switch. Yet even these reprieves could not be savoured without guilt. They were so accustomed to being in a committed state of readiness that sleep was not to be trusted. 'When I sleep, I feel like I'm cheating,' said one recruit.

Looking back, they could hardly remember what they'd done from one day to the next. It was almost seamless – as soon as one evolution was done another was set. A gruelling two-hour gym circuit followed by five and a half hours of finning, say. Or mundane speed-dressing drills followed by a long-distance canoe paddle and portage followed by a ten-kilometre pack march or a stretcher carry, where an eighty-kilogram load had to be shouldered up and down rugged hills for hours. And all the while the supervisors, the chief and the shrink were messing with their heads, issuing repetitive tasks, sending them on aimless quests, giving them a rev-up when they were going slow and handing out push-ups like speeding tickets. The whole ordeal was passing by relentlessly in a painful, excoriating haze. Somewhere along the line, the key demand of the course had changed. For all the incessant physical activity, it was now primarily a mind game.

To get even this far they had had to be extremely fit and ultra-determined. There was barely an ounce of body fat between them. With resting heart rates in the forties or fifties, they were fitter than just about everyone else in the navy, PT instructors included. They took a great deal of pride, both as individuals and as a team, in being able to handle anything thrown at them. But after so much punishment they'd come to know that their survival depended primarily on their mental strength. Even the strongest, most athletic among them were seized by crippling doubt. At times they felt certain that they couldn't make it through the next PT session. They knew full well there was no such thing as being nursed through CDAT, yet still the dehumanising absence of recognition, praise and encouragement would disorientate and confuse them. They would be busting a gut and some jerk would be in their face telling them they were slacking off. Their brain would drift into dangerous territory. *Should I punch this fucker out? Is this ever going to end? I don't think I can make it! Even if I do, maybe I will fail. What will I do then? How could I face these guys if I fail and get left behind?* The pain was deeply personal, yet everyone knew it and they faced this demon together. Something of a code had developed between them: don't give anything less than one hundred per cent. That was the only way failure could be accepted.

The scope of thought and conversation was reduced to how they were going, whether or not they'd get through and what they needed to do to last the distance. There was always some lighthearted piss-taking over their grim lot – gallows humour – but their spirits swung wildly up and down. Doubt could hit any of them hard at any time. A dejected mate would be urged not to quit but to complete just one more evolution and see how he felt after. Under the cold, efficient system of culling, bonds stronger than mateship were forged: a warrior brotherhood. The individual was a collective concern and vice versa. You never gave up, and you never gave up on your brother. A pure survival mechanism was kicking in: the tribe helped individuals transform debilitating fear into accomplishment. The disheartened became proud again and stood ready for more.

Physical discomfort had ceased to matter. One way or another, all the candidates were suffering – burning muscles, chafing, blisters, cramps, tears, persistent aches, strains and rashes. They practically bathed in liniment. They had so much Elastoplast stuck to their bodies you'd think they would fall apart without it. The chafing was like some rampant virus. To fight it they wore protective tape behind the neck, in the crook of knees, around ankles and feet, over nipples and under armpits. Exercise, wet clothes, wetsuits and sand were at war with their skin. In some cases, the rashes cut though to the flesh. One candidate had to keep a woollen sock over his wedding tackle.

Sometimes all the will and tape in the world can't hold the body together. On day six, Number 7's gave out. He should have been on the previous CDAT but sinus surgery forced him to postpone. He saw his original group of mates go through, and all he wanted was to be hot on their heels: pass CDAT, get rated as a clearance diver and join them out on a team. But after a PT session on day five he found he couldn't stretch his right quad. He spent the morning of day six with the medics while the other lads cracked on. The quad was torn. If he continued on he risked a haemorrhage, so the medics pulled him off course. If he was lucky, he would be allowed to do CDAT again. That decision depended on whether he'd convinced the assessors that he could cut it, and there was no certainty of that. He had to wait till the end of the course to find out.

Number 6 was the next to go. He was a tall, solid unit who had once wanted to convert his junior rep rugby league into a pro career. To earn money, he worked as a builder and moonlighted as a bouncer. One night a brawl broke out in the bar. He rushed in and a pisshead took a swing, so he dropped the guy and kept him down by putting a foot on his chest. Another punter came at him and Number 6 managed to subdue him as well. That's when he felt the knife slide out of his leg. He put his hand to his groin area to stop the gushing blood. His strength began to drain away. His mates came to his aid and he was rushed to hospital.

The knife had missed the femoral artery by two millimetres. The incident gave Number 6 pause to think about his life. Since having to let go of his football ambitions, he'd yearned for something more exciting and challenging, but playing zookeeper to yobbos wasn't exactly what he had in mind. He wanted to do something that had purpose. He had three uncles who'd been in the SAS, and one of them suggested he check out the military. So Number 6 went along to a JOES day, or enlistment day, intending to join the army and follow in the footsteps of his uncles, but once he was told about clearance diving that all changed. Being a keen diver and spearfisherman, Number 6 believed clearance diving was the best fit. And that seemed to be true enough: he was proving to be one of the strongest candidates on course. But late on day six, he slipped on the freshly mopped galley floor and slammed to the ground, flat on his back. The force of the blow paralysed him. The longer he lay there, the more serious his injury seemed. Ultimately, he was able to get to his feet, but his back had seized up so fiercely he was unable to continue CDAT and was pulled off course.

Number 20, the desert ultra-marathoner, was next. He succumbed to a back injury. Both these latter candidates were prepared to do CDAT again, but now they were told that, pending final assessment, they still might be passed and allowed through to the basic clearance diving course.

Until recently, that would never happen. There were three things you had to do to pass CDAT. First, you had to finish the course. Second, your overall performance had to be solid. And third, you had to be the right fit: a capable individual as well as a team player. There was no doubt that Numbers 6 and 20 were well on track to satisfying two of these criteria, but by old-school standards they had failed. Veteran clearance divers might shake their heads at such leniency, but times have changed. It wasn't Numbers 6 and 20 who revised the rules. They would now have to wait for the assessors' verdict. Meanwhile, their vests were taken to the diving school launch and hung on a rail alongside the others. Two more scalps to the door bitch.

The remaining eleven candidates carried on, never knowing what was coming up next. Not every task was exhausting. Some, like speed-dressing drills, were mind-numbingly boring. In one instance they were told to form up in their PT gear and ordered to be in their wetsuits in five minutes. These were short-arm steamers over which they pulled long-sleeve jackets that fastened from below with a beaver-tail flap. Their wetsuits were damp and sandy, so often in use that they never got the chance to dry. As the recruits raced through the drill, they helped each other out until all were ready, standing at attention with fins tucked under their left arms. The chief looked at his watch and told them they were thirty-five seconds slow. Not good enough. He ordered them to undress to their swimmers again and 'show some urgency'.

Immediately, they started contorting to free themselves of their wetsuits and eventually reformed at attention in their sluggos, vests and water bottle (their constant companion). They were all identically dressed except for Number 9 – he was wearing bicycle shorts. The dress kits are not suggestions or outfits that you can accessorise and make your own. They are one-for-all uniforms. Adding insult to injury, Number 9 was chewing gum. One of the petty officers had ordered him to get rid of the gum before. The clear warnings about 'violations' seemed to have fallen on deaf ears. This was Number 9's second attempt at CDAT. Last time round he finished the course but was failed because he was deemed to be unsuitable. They'd told him he was too 'individualistic', 'thought of himself too much' and 'lacked a bit of teamwork'. He said that after being failed he had shed a few tears, hated the world and himself for a couple of weeks, but had then restarted his training regime with the explicit aim of passing on his second attempt. But if Number 9 had really learned, he wouldn't have been standing there in bicycle shorts, chewing gum. He would go on to finish CDAT for a second time, and for a second time he would be failed.

The squad repeated their dress drills over and over again. Defying the drudgery of it all, they revved each other up, helped the stragglers and called out items to check. Their times came down and down until, on about the tenth change of dress, they went from sluggos to wetsuits in one minute forty-three. By then the chief had given them only one minute, so he sent them off to do another gruelling hour of PT.

That night, they were woken at three. They had five minutes to get out of their bunks, into their wetsuits and down to the end of the wharf. Into the black water they jumped again. They linked arms to form a line and began kicking towards open water. Rain began to fall and a cold breeze lifted. The big launch chugged slowly behind, the chief keeping a constant eye out. At one point, he stabbed the torchlight at them.

'Who coughed?' he demanded. Coughing might indicate a candidate was suffering from saltwater aspiration. Fin for hours in an exhausted state and you are going to swallow sea water and get some into your lungs too. The inhaled salt water will draw fluid from your body into your lungs, and soon enough you could have lung failure. The candidates convinced the chief no one had coughed.

Along the shore beautiful homes reeled past, some glowing warmly from within. On board the launch, in the cold drizzle, the talk was about sharks. There were plenty about, but at this hour of night they posed minimal risk to the swimmers. The diving branch had had to make changes since Paul de Gelder lost a hand and a leg to a bull shark at Garden Island. The hours around dawn and dusk were now avoided.

Occasionally, the chief stuck his head out of the cabin and without speaking flashed his torch twice at the squad. Immediately, a count-off commenced. As they called out their numbers in the darkness, only the swimmers' faces and the cyalume sticks attached to their shoulders could be seen. And they would keep kicking away until they were told to stop, until they knew they'd rounded that next corner and were one more fraction closer to finishing. As they headed up Pittwater towards the devilish blinking eye of Lion Island, perhaps they had begun to wonder for the thousandth time if they really wanted to be a clearance diver, and for the thousandth time pushed all doubt aside.

TWO

BEATING HITLER'S SECRET WEAPON

CLEARANCE DIVING CAME into being because of the mine. It was a task borne of dire necessity: to dispose of – defuse, delouse, defeat, dismantle, render safe, pacify, neuter, rip the blasted guts out of – Hitler's diabolically brilliant sea mines. Diving was first and foremost a delivery mechanism to pit man against these mines under water. Mine disposal was no job for the faint-hearted; it had to be done safely, with steady courage. Success didn't just save lives in the immediate vicinity; it saved them in the future by exposing enemy secrets, and at one point it changed the course of the Second World War. Britain had to retrieve mines *intact* in order to scrutinise their workings. The need could not have been more acute because the Royal Navy, like much of Britain's leadership, had been caught napping. While they remained jammed in a First World War mindset, Germany was busy forging the future, propelling mine warfare into a new and terrifying age. And by this disadvantage alone Britain found herself facing defeat within weeks of the war's beginning.

≈

One evening in London, a young lieutenant in the Royal Navy named Alec Dennis stepped out for a drink. It was late 1939 and Dennis's injured ship, HMS *Griffin*, had had to rush up the Thames and into dock for repairs. Her crew was gifted ten days ashore. For all that Dennis savoured on his night out, the experience as a whole didn't sit well with him. Life was oddly, almost offensively, normal.

'London seemed to be on a peacetime footing,' he wrote in his journal. 'Food and drink were plentiful, nightclubs full of people and blue smoke.'

Dennis, who months later captured the Enigma machine codebooks that allowed Britain to decrypt German communiqués, didn't begrudge anyone having a good time in the face of dire circumstances. But he was appalled to find the belief that the looming storm had stalled, or was even lying dormant, was so widely held. His blood really boiled, though, to hear people dismiss this new great conflict as the 'phoney war'.

Since Germany's invasion of Poland in early September 1939, the dismal gears of world war had groaned to life again, yet so far hell had not been unleashed, at least not on British soil. King George VI had warned ominously over the radio that 'war can no longer be confined to the battlefield'. Air raids were expected, as were hordes of German paratroopers. City children had been sent to the country and gas masks had been issued widely. But the *Luftwaffe* had failed to appear.

Britain had actually been bracing for war since Hitler invaded Czechoslovakia a year earlier. Her armed forces had been deployed to the Continent, and yet no major battles had erupted. There was no front line to report from. Britain's war was all talk and no action, apparently. People grew accustomed to stand-by mode.

For sailors like Dennis, though, there was no waiting. The war had begun quickly and in earnest. Germany's initial strike weapon was not the U-boat or the bomber, but the mine, and the shallow channels skirting Britain were soon littered with them. But this was no ordinary contact mine, the black-horned devil that lurked at hull-depth on the end of a sinker; it was some other mysterious beast that could elude British minesweepers. To sail the English Channel and the North Sea at the time was to play Russian roulette. Dennis knew full well what it felt like to be floating on such perilous waters. Like all sailors, he was mindful to walk with his knees bent, such was the unholy fear of being thunderstruck from below. Only a few nights before his London jaunt, Dennis witnessed the horror of the new mine at work.

The *Griffin* was part of a North Sea patrol flotilla. One night, having just completed a patrol, the ships were ordered straight back out of Harwich Harbour to chase four German destroyers spotted off the Dutch coast. The *Griffin* led the convoy with a fellow destroyer, HMS *Gipsy*, a minute behind. Suddenly, there was an 'almighty bang and flash of light', recorded Dennis. A mine had detonated directly underneath the *Gipsy*, and its blast broke the 1400-ton warship in half, 'right between the funnels'. The *Griffin* moved in to pick up the survivors.

'Mingled with the cries of the drowning men was the mournful tolling of the channel bell buoy,' Dennis wrote. 'A fitting requiem for the first of our flotilla to go.'

Cruelly, Dennis's flotilla had been sent to hunt phantoms. The four destroyers reported were in fact the *Griffin* and company on their earlier patrol. The RAF observer had mistaken them for German ships.

The mine that sank the *Gipsy* was a magnetic mine. Delivered by a German plane, it had descended via parachute, dangling by the tail like a pendant, and had sunk to the bottom of the harbour's access channel. It was a ground mine, designed to rest on the sea floor rather than 'float' like a contact mine. A ship did not have to touch a magnetic mine to detonate it. This new mine effectively took note of the magnetic field around it, and when a passing ship disturbed that field it blew. The device was rigged to fire just as its magnetometer came off its peak, so the blast would hit right in midships. The mine typically contained a ton of high explosive, and the bubble created by the blast quickly transformed into a battering ram of water that shot straight up, striking the ship with enough force to lift it out of the water. (A sailor on the cruiser HMS *Belfast*, which was hit by a magnetic mine the same day as the *Gipsy*, told of being thrown five metres skywards.) The panels of ships at the time were held together by rivets and the force of the water was so violent that gaps opened between the plates everywhere. Water poured in and the ship quickly sank, its back broken. The British had suspected the Germans were using magnetic mines because they could find no evidence of direct contact on the hulls of damaged ships like the *Belfast*. But they had no way to collect, identify or deal with such a weapon: all they had was conjecture.

Before the war Hitler had boasted of possessing a 'secret weapon' that could not be foiled. There were rumours that the Nazis had developed a death ray. But this secret weapon was in fact the magnetic mine. For all Hitler's talk, the *Kriegsmarine* was surprised to find the British so vulnerable. The Brits themselves had used magnetic mines against Germany late in the previous war, and so the Germans, expecting more of the same, had raced to develop countermeasures for their own ships. The Royal Navy, however, had not followed through in any such regard. Their sweepers were only able to catch the old horned mine, cutting the mooring cable so that the mine popped up to the surfaced and could be destroyed by gunfire. Being unsweepable made the magnetic mine illegal under international law. Hitler, of course, answered to no law. Germany righteously claimed to be targeting her enemy's warships, but the real target was Britain's lifeblood: the trade vessel. In the First World War, the Kaiser had used U-boats to effect a crippling blockade of Britain, and now the same tactic was being employed by different means. The effect was devastating. Almost 60,000 tons in Allied merchant shipping were lost in September and October of 1939. Double that amount was lost in November alone.

'A new and formidable danger threatened our life,' wrote Winston Churchill in his memoirs. Churchill was First Lord of the Admiralty at the time and acutely aware of the imperative to solve the mysteries of this underwater menace. 'Every day hundreds of ships went in and out of British harbours, and our survival depended on their movement. Hitler's experts may well have told him that this form of attack would compass our ruin. Luckily he began on a small scale, and with limited stocks and manufacturing capacity.'

The magnetic mine was without doubt the single greatest threat to Britain. Starved of fuel, food and arms, she faced the prospect of early capitulation.

Churchill was grateful for the relatively low production run of the mine. Also working in Britain's favour was the disharmony between the *Luftwaffe* and the *Kriegsmarine*. The *Luftwaffe* could proudly drop the new mine on Britain's doorstep without having to navigate Britain's own defensive mine fields. To the German navy, though, this method of delivery was far too imprecise for such a highly valued weapon: a pilot had no control of the mine once it left the aircraft; the parachute was at the mercy of the wind. A ship or U-boat could lay that mine with the sureness of placing cutlery on a table. *Kriegsmarine* fears that their secret weapon would drop straight into the enemy's lap were justified. Weeks into the war, pilot error gave Britain a lucky break.

At ten o'clock on the moonless night of 22 November, a German pilot flying over the mouth of the Thames in driving rain and under fire dropped two parachute mines too close to shore. They landed in the shallow water off

Shoeburyness. Sentries noted where the mines fell and informed Admiralty.

This was the call Lieutenant Commander John Ouvry had been waiting for. As the leading mine disposal technician at HMS *Vernon*, a Royal Navy depot that specialised in underwater weapons, Ouvry had put a lot of thought into how he would go about tackling a magnetic mine. It was, of course, all theory because no one had ever done it. He was well aware that *Vernon*'s boffins were desperate to get their hands on an intact specimen so they could reverse-engineer its architecture and develop countermeasures, and he knew full well it was his job was to secure one. The trouble was, up to this point, you only knew a magnetic mine was present after it had blown up one of your ships.

By three o'clock, Ouvry and his colleague, Lieutenant Commander Roger Lewis, had arrived at Southend with orders to recover the mine at all costs. They trudged out and inspected the dark, insidious lump under torchlight. Two metres long and as thick as a keg, the mine weighed 550 kilograms. Stabilising horns protruded from its snubbed nose, and there was an empty compartment at the tail where the parachute had sprung from. There was a round fitting near the nose. This was the fuse, the gateway into the detonation system. The men could see that a four-pin spanner was needed to unscrew the outer ring that held the fuse in place. They didn't have such a tool, so Lewis took an imprint of the ring and sent it to a local workshop to have one made.

The next day the second mine was spotted 300 metres

away. Ouvry decided that he and Lewis would not tackle the first mine together. Instead, Ouvry would take Chief Petty Officer Charles Baldwin to assist him while Lewis watched Ouvry's every move through binoculars. Then Lewis would take the next mine with Able Seaman Archibald Vearncombe.

'We fixed on a definite sequence of events, which he [Lewis] could clearly observe from the distance, in case of a mistake upon my part,' Ouvry wrote in his report. Ouvry would signal after completing each stage of the agreed plan. That way, if he was blown to smithereens, Lewis would know exactly where to deviate when dealing with his mine.

Low tide came in the early afternoon. Ouvry emptied his pockets of everything metallic, gathered up his toolkit, which now included a brass four-pin spanner, and strode out towards a mine powerful enough to snap a warship in half. All shipping in the vicinity had come to a standstill and was awaiting word of his success or the thunder of his failure. So much rested on Ouvry salvaging this mine. If unchecked, the Nazi stranglehold of Britain's sea lanes, which already had some parliamentarians wanting to broker a peace deal, would have brought Britain to her knees. By any measure, the shipping losses could not be sustained, and there was no telling when the Brits would get another chance to examine the culprit.

Ouvry had no idea what this mine was designed to respond to. It could be magnetic. It could be an acoustic mine, a noise-sensitive weapon that was reportedly on the German production line. It could be induced to fire in some other way known only to its makers. Whatever the mine's temperament, taming it was Ouvry's job.

As Ouvry and Baldwin advanced, Britain had her second stroke of luck. Ouvry's eye was caught by a shining piece of metal that lay half-buried in the mud. He picked it up and examined the object: a newly machined brass rod. Ouvry wondered if it had come off the nearby mine. When he reached the weapon he saw there was a hole into which the rod fitted perfectly. *That's probably the safety pin*, he thought to himself. But he couldn't be absolutely sure the mine was safe. His every move would be breaking new ground. He got to work.

With all the delicate control he could muster, Ouvry fitted the spanner and began unscrewing the outer ring. Next, he cautiously extracted the item that he took to be the detonator. Inside were small discs of explosive, confirming his hunch. Believing the worst had passed, he called for assistance to roll the mine over so he could access the components he could see through the outer ring. Resuming his work, he was alarmed to find a second, larger detonator and realised that this was actually part of the main firing system. Pressing on, he continued to remove every item that might trigger the main charge – some 300 kilograms of high explosive – until finally he was done. After two and a half hours bent over the mine, Ouvry was confident it was now harmless. A rush of elation and relief swept through him. It wasn't every day that you got to change the course of a war.

The men, the mine casing and all its parts were taken back to *Vernon*. 'I welcomed them with enthusiasm,' wrote Churchill. 'I gathered together eighty or a hundred officers and officials in our largest room, and a thrilled audience listened to the tale, deeply conscious of all that was at stake. From this moment the whole position was transformed.'

On 19 December, King George VI decorated Ouvry and Lewis with the Distinguished Service Order. Baldwin and Vearncombe received the Distinguished Service Medal. These were the first Royal Navy decorations of the war. Many believed Ouvry deserved nothing less than the Victoria Cross, the military's highest award for bravery. He got the DSO, however, because his heroic act was deemed not to have taken place 'in the face of the enemy'.

Ouvry's recovery job soon led to a remedy. It was discovered that by placing an electrically charged wire cable around a ship, its magnetic field could be neutralised. Suddenly, a demand for these 'degaussing girdles' skyrocketed. At one stage, 1900 kilometres of wire cable were being fitted to ships every week. Immunity at last.

But the war was only just getting started. Mine warfare was now an arms race all on its own: action and reaction drove the scientific mind to conceive of more sophisticated behaviours for the mines. It fell to the analytical mind and courageous heart to thwart them.

When Lieutenant Dennis went out drinking in London that night in November, he found himself wondering how those 'phoney war' subscribers would like a taste of the war as he knew it. 'I wished some of them could try a few wet, cold nights off the Gabbard [Shoal, just off the Suffolk coast], get blown up and go for a swim. Perhaps some of them did, later.' In a matter of months, though, the sight of fighters and bombers overhead was so familiar that boys could identify the model of a plane by the drone of its engines. War had strayed from the battlefield and was now crashing down upon Britain's cities and civilians. Dennis's words had proved prophetic, at least in regard to people knowing, feeling and fearing the terrifying power of the mine. The mines he had come to know were no longer just lying in wait under water or in tidal zones, they were being dropped on London and other cities, landing in the middle of housing estates, streets and parks. By then, just about everyone in Britain knew what a parachute mine was. And nobody talked about the war being phoney.

≈

It is said that John Ouvry being denied a Victoria Cross led to the creation of the 'civilian VC': the George Cross. This new medal, honouring deeds *not* performed under fire, was more than that: it symbolised the communion between an unexpectedly popular king and his people. King George VI had been ruling since 1936, when Britain began rearming in response to Hitler's furious militarisation. He was thrust onto the throne, filling the void left by his elder brother's scandalous abdication. Up until then, this inconsequential royal, who stammered and shunned the limelight, was not credited with any capacity to rule and possessed no desire to do so. But once in the hot seat, the 'reluctant king' proved to be an admirable, compassionate and independently minded monarch. Throughout the Blitz he refused to flee the capital, staying put with his family, sheltering when the sirens howled, living on rations and patching his clothes. The George Cross was very much his pet project. It came out early in the *Luftwaffe* assault on London, as though to greet with due recognition the most heroic deeds sprouting from the rubble, fire and carnage. Introduced on 24 September 1940, the king made the George Cross equal to the Victoria Cross as the highest mark of valour, except that it was open to anyone, citizen or serviceman. The George Medal was also established, falling directly below the GC in order of merit. During the entire war, around 120 George Crosses were won, but only eight individuals won both the King's cross and medal. Three of this latter group were Australian – naval volunteers named John Stuart Mould, Hugh Randall Syme and Leon Verdi Goldsworthy. A fourth, George Gosse, won the George Cross. These four men are the forefathers of today's Australian clearance divers. They learned on the job to become cutting-edge divers and masters of mine disposal, pioneering the core skills of their modern-day kin. By war's end, they ranked among the most highly decorated men of any service, of any country.

Mould and Syme were the first to make their mark. Both were recruited for the Royal Navy by the Australian Navy, which wasn't hiring. The 'Yachtsmen Scheme' called for men with sailing experience to apply. They were assessed in Australia and then shipped to Mother England. Mould was from Sydney, and he was very much a social sailor – he didn't like a swell to spill his drink. He had actually enlisted with the army but then changed over to navy while recovering from pneumonia. Syme, whose family owned and ran *The Age* in Melbourne, was a true yachtie. Both men were made probationary officers simply because they were over thirty. (At thirty-seven, Syme was seven years older than Mould.) Along with twenty-two other such officers, they boarded the P&O steamer *Strathnaver* and left HMAS *Cerberus* in mid-September 1940. The shipload carried another 150 naval volunteers who, being under thirty, were taken on as 'ratings', or regular seaman. When they reached Liverpool six weeks later their ship was unable to dock. The *Luftwaffe* had dropped mines into the Mersey overnight, paralysing the port. The *Strathnaver* had to stand off for the night and from here the Australians got their first look at the war.

Air-raid sirens hit full cry as German bombers tore in overhead, dogged by anti-aircraft fire and spotlights. The air filled with the erratic percussion of bombs, and red flashes lit up facets of architecture. By the end, Liverpool was smouldering red. Watching the horrific spectacle from the water, Mould and Syme may have tried to imagine the kind of combat experience that awaited them – at sea with enemy planes zeroing in and all manner of hell erupting all around them. Never in their wildest dreams would they have thought that their war would be an intimate, solitary and often silent one, that their destiny was about to be entwined with the likes of those mines that lurked somewhere beneath them in the Mersey, the very menace that was holding them at bay.

After *Strathnaver* finally docked, the probationary officers headed to HMS *King Alfred*, a naval base near Brighton, for six weeks of training. Mould and Syme never finished the course. Halfway through, a signal came from Admiralty, the Royal Navy's high command in London, calling for volunteers to undertake 'special duties ashore'. The Head of Torpedoes and Mines had heard that some Australians had arrived. He figured that they would be up for anything, taking them as being equal parts carefree and courageous. All but two of the Australians volunteered and four were chosen: Mould, Syme, James Kessack and Dudley Reid. They had no idea what they had got themselves into, but in due course they found out: they were going to be trained to dispose of mines.

'They were more or less put into it,' remembered Noel Cashford, who passed away aged 88 a few months after being interviewed. Cashford was a Royal Navy volunteer who as a young lieutenant was taught mine disposal by Mould and Syme. 'But typical of the Aussies in those days, they made the best of it. They said, "We don't really want this damned job but we'll stick with it." '

Of course, none of the four had a clue about mines. They were transferred to the Rendering Mines Safe (RMS) section at *Vernon* for a crash course. *Vernon* was located at Portsmouth, the home of the Royal Navy. People called Portsmouth 'Pompey' for various reasons but for sailors the nickname referred to the pomp and ceremony of a living antiquity. Mould, for one, grew to love the place. Being a Sydneysider, he naturally thought Portsmouth harbour was ridiculous – so small and narrow-necked – but it came to represent all that he admired about Britain. He liked to sit on the jetty and watch destroyers lead their flotillas out on offensive patrols, 'A-Hunting We Will Go' blaring from the lead ship's loudhailers.

'The same spirit was still there in those ships of the Royal Navy as had been so long before,' he wrote. 'Sailing out into the unknown the same way that Nelson and so many seamen had sailed before.'

The mine game had evolved since Ouvry's feat at Shoeburyness. Britain's response to Hitler's secret weapon – degaussing girdles – came swiftly. Germany had expected them to take years, not months, to find a remedy. Suddenly, the need to gain another lethal advantage grew all the more urgent. The knowledge gained by Ouvry, his colleagues and the boffins at *Vernon* had been formalised into courses – and RMS was hungry for graduates. Actually, the RMS team operating out of London was given a new, non-specific title, for security reasons: the Land Incident Section (LIS). As the Nazis began dropping sea mines all over Britain, this unit suddenly found itself in desperate need of extra hands.

There was another development, the graduates were told: the Germans were out to kill them, specifically. Their mines were now being fitted with anti-recovery devices. Only two months before the Australians arrived, a mine that appeared to be standard was stored in *Vernon*'s examination shed. Defused and with its main charge removed, the mine was considered harmless. A petty officer returned to complete his inspection and undid the screws that held a panel at the rear. He moved the panel only slightly. A whirring, like that of a wind-up toy, came from within the mine, followed by a blinding flash and blast. The petty officer and five other men in the shed were killed. The man standing behind the petty officer, who had watched his every move, survived.

After the mine debris was pieced together, it was discovered that a booby-trap had been fitted to protect the secrecy of a new delay mechanism, called a 'clicker', that was designed to foil British minesweepers. The sweepers targeted magnetic mines by trawling a device that mimicked a ship's magnetic influence, tricking the mine into detonating at a safe distance behind. But with a six-click switch, the sweeper could trip the device up to five times and give the all-clear to shipping, only to have the next ship to pass over set the mine off.

Ten days after the fatal explosion in the shed, a German bomber flew right over *Vernon* and dropped two mines fifteen kilometres inland from the coast. This was highly unusual at the time since the *Luftwaffe* had only been targeting waterways. As luck would have it, one of the mines blew open on impact. What the RMS men found inside turned their blood cold. There was no main charge at all, just three smaller but still lethal charges, each fitted to a booby-trap. This was not a mine built to sink a ship; it was a lure, custom made to assassinate RMS officers. Mine warfare had just become very personal. Then it turned indiscriminate.

Since 1936, Britain had feared Hitler would invade. In mid-1940 that doomsday scenario began to play out. The German leader had hoped he could talk, and choke, Chamberlain's Britain into standing by while he steamrolled Europe. But once Churchill was installed as Prime Minister in May, Britain's countenance firmed radically. There would be no peace deals and no stepping aside: every word Churchill had for Hitler was bare-fisted. Unable to ignore an actively hostile Britain, Hitler was compelled to try and smash belligerence into submission. He launched Operation Sealion, the German battle plan for the invasion of Britain, with an ominous first phase: the crippling of the Royal Air Force.

So the Battle of Britain began, with *Luftwaffe* bombers targeting military assets and infrastructure. The RAF didn't just defend, they launched bombing raids of their own. But when German bombs strayed onto purely civilian targets in London, the gentleman's agreement was off – Churchill promptly ordered a series of audacious bombing raids on Berlin, an act that so surprised and outraged Hitler that he replied with unrestrained force. The RAF, which by now was down to a few serviceable aircraft operating from airfields that could barely take any more hammering, was suddenly reprieved as the *Luftwaffe* rounded on London. And so, on 7 September 1940, the Battle of Britain morphed into the Blitz.

This was the scenario into which Mould, Syme, Kessack and Reid were cast: Britain in the throes of total war. Bombers and fighter planes by the hundreds passed overhead each night. Fresh news of death and destruction appeared every day. Then, in mid-September reports came of extraordinarily large blasts in London, Kent and Essex. Hundreds of houses were destroyed and many residents had been killed by German parachute mines. Unlike a heavy bomb that penetrated the ground and spent a lot of its force making a crater, the blast of the softer landing parachute mine could radiate to full effect. Word of the doomsday press coverage and fearful public outrage reached Germany. These mines had delivered such a hammerblow to the morale of London residents that the Germans were encouraged to use more. Nothing served the cause of terror better. Air Force Commander-in-Chief Goering felt he had the means to break Britain's spirit once and for all. *Luftwaffe* raids would now be laced with mine-layers.

People didn't know what to make of the parachute mines at first. Amid all the incendiaries and other conventional bombs, an observer would hear a parachute thump into bloom and see it fall to earth, carrying a huge stump of a thing. Individuals would try and move these beasts out of the road or salvage the parachutes – the cloth and the cords, prized as belts and sources of yarn, sold well on the black market – only to be blown up. Eventually awareness spread and people knew to give the mines a wide berth. It became common, then, to try and detonate them by rifle shot before they landed. These mines were generally called, logically but inaccurately, 'land mines' and recognised as the most insidious weapon to fall from the sky. Sometimes buildings would trip a mine's magnetic sensor and it would explode just above ground. Packed with up to 700 kilograms of explosives, their destructive power was unrivalled.

'I saw some of the damage they'd done, and you wouldn't believe it,' said Cashford. 'If you stood in the middle, for a quarter-mile radius you'd see houses knocked down. Some were still standing, but there wouldn't be a window in place. The roof, in many cases, was just blown off. I don't know if you've seen pictures of Hiroshima in Japan but it looked very similar to that. And there was nothing we could do about it.'

On 29 November 1940, a parachute mine exploded on top

of a boiler room in Liverpool in which 300 people were sheltering. The building collapsed and was flooded with boiling
water. In the end, 166 civilians were killed. A mother who
lost four children in this nightmarish incident did not speak
for six months. Churchill later described the tragedy as 'the
worst single [civilian] incident of the war'.

As many as a third of all parachute mines, though, failed to
detonate upon landing. It would become Mould and Syme's
job to go out and deal with them. They had joined the navy
expecting to be posted on a ship, a torpedo boat at the very
least. Yet here they were with their purpose directed inland,
getting intimate with bombs that could vaporise them as
quick as you could blink.

At *Vernon*, the workings of magnetic mines, though, were
explained to them. When not armed, the mine was in a pas-
sive state. When armed, or cocked, it became 'alive' and
began to 'listen'. It would take its reading of the surrounding
area and feel for any disturbance. You only had to remove a
nearby star picket to trigger an active magnetic mine. A set of
keys a foot away could push the sensor needle far enough to
close the firing circuit. The men were told about the mechanical fuses that whirred when they were tripped. If they ever
heard such a sound they had, at best, seventeen seconds to
run for cover. But you never really knew how much time you
had because the fuses were so damned stop-start twitchy. If
you were hunched over a mine and the fuse started up, you
may only have a second to live.

Step by step, they were taught how to dismantle a
mine safely, a job that required the patience of a spy and a

pickpocket's touch. There were tools of the trade to become familiar with. There were techniques to learn, such as burning down a mine's main charge using thermite. The primary goal, almost a mantra, was to recover the mine intact. Then, after a couple of weeks, school was out. Mould, Syme, Kessack and Reid were now mine-recovery officers.

Inside the Admiralty building in London they were each interviewed by Captain C. N. E. Currey, the man who had signalled for volunteers. Currey, a South African, was a perceptive and industrious commander. He was also a straight shooter. He reminded Syme of the risks, that he and his fellow countrymen were filling dead men's shoes, replacing victims of a lethal cat-and-mouse game. He told Syme he should pull out immediately if he nursed any doubts. This was an offer a commander no doubt feels he must make while never wanting or expecting it to be accepted: it served Currey's conscience more than anything. Syme insisted he wanted in. Currey asked him why.

'I don't know, sir,' Syme replied, 'except that I don't like the idea of being maimed or messed up. I'm told that in this business the end is sharp and clean.'

The other three gave Currey the same answer for different reasons.

'No two men came at it the same,' wrote Ivan Southall in *Softly Tread the Brave*. 'Syme was perfectly honest; he couldn't determine his attitude and didn't know where to begin. Only one thing he knew for certain and that was his fear. Mould, too, was unsure of his emotions. By nature spirited and carefree, now he was frightened. He was disconcerted and not himself. Red [Kessack] was unduly boisterous, in his own way trying to stiffen his morale and the morale of his friends. There were unguarded moments when Red's face was blank and long-drawn. Dudley Reid was there by concession only. He had felt duty-bound to volunteer, but still wanted to go to sea. He would honour his obligation until he had done what he considered to be his fair share.'

Mould hardly slept that first week in London. The fear of the task ahead was itself enough to keep his mind racing, but there was no getting used to the apocalyptic din and shudder of the nightly raids. It was some weird kind of hell: a bitter winter closing in on a burning metropolis. Launching from new bases in occupied territory across the Channel, the *Luftwaffe* was dumping millions of tonnes of ordnance on Britain, having expanded its Blitz targets from London to Coventry, Glasgow, Liverpool and more cities besides.

Mould had nothing much to do but wait for the call. He went through the drills he was taught at *Vernon* over and over again. In theory, he could strip a mine blindfolded. In reality, there was a good chance he would not get that far. In the booming of the biggest shells beyond the walls, he could hear the likely the sound of his own death.

His first mine was waiting for him in a muddy field in Kent. Half-buried, it stood in the morning mist like a tombstone. An experienced disposal officer was with him – his nurse on his learner's job – but as they walked towards the mine on this cold, damp morning, his companion stopped. Here, 120-odd metres from the mine, they dug a shallow pit. From this point on, Mould was on his own. He doubted he could reach the pit in seventeen seconds, if he had that long. Not in this mud. He picked up the heavy tool bag – it weighed 30 kilos – and walked down range.

Mould couldn't stop trembling. Not so long ago he was an architect, father and divorcee in Sydney. Now he was in the middle of a freshly ploughed field near London having to dissect a mine that might blow the moment he touched it. A couple of days earlier an RMS man had been killed by a mine like this in such a field. All up, that fate awaited about one in three.

If Mould was out of place, so too was the mine. The parachute mines were built to end up on the sea floor. An impact fuse had been fitted as a workaround to make this naval weapon work like bomb. If the mine landed on dry ground, the timer would run down, the detonator would fire and the mine would explode. The bomb fuse could also be seen as a self-destruct mechanism to protect the German armourer's secrets. Same with any booby-trap that might be fitted. So although Mould and his mine were on land, they were engaged in a duel that represented the leading edge of the battle between ships and mines at sea. By successfully taking his mine to pieces, Mould could reveal something new about how the enemy was thinking. And any fresh insight would sharpen their minesweepers' effectiveness, and save untold money and lives by keeping ships afloat and a nation adequately fed and armed.

Mould started with the impact fuse, because it was a dangerous unknown. For some reason it had failed to go off. He had to remove it before the rundown clock started, or restarted again if it had jammed. At any moment it could spring back to life. That's when Mould would have to stand up and sprint for the pit.

The fuse had a safety mechanism, operated by water pressure. Water could pour into the fuse chamber, and when enough pressure was created it pushed a small diaphragm that in turn lodged a safety pin that disabled the fuse. This way, if the mine landed in water and reached a depth of four metres, the impact fuse would be made redundant, leaving detonation to the mine's main firing system. Once the mine is submerged, a salt plug dissolves, which starts the hydrostatic arming clock of the mine. Now the mine can do what it was meant to do – wait for a ship to flip its sensor and set off a rapidly escalating detonation chain. A strong enough magnetic signal would close an electric circuit powered by a small battery. The current would then fire the detonator. The detonator blast would fire the booster charge, also called the primer. The explosion of the primer would produce a concussive force powerful enough to set off the main charge, which in Mould's case was about 700 kilograms of TNT.

To mimic the pressure of water filling the fuse chamber, Mould pumped air into it using a pressure horn. This was a modified car horn that could be pumped up tight and then fitted over the fuse. The air pressure from the horn would lodge the safety pin and hold it there. Trembling and nauseous from the stress, Mould tried screwing the pressure horn onto the fuse. The only sound was his laboured breathing. Once, he fumbled the tool and it fell clanking against the mine. He braced to flee. No noise came from within. The fuse had not started. He resumed his work until he heard the click of the safety pin lodging. He then took his four-pin spanner, unscrewed the outer ring and drew the fuse out. Thankfully, there wasn't a Zus 40, the anti-handling device, attached to the end of it. The Zus 40 was a second fuse fitted directly behind the impact fuse and was hidden from view. If the impact fuse is yanked out, the Zus 40 goes off.

Next, Mould had to remove the primer mechanism. The holding ring squeaked as he strained against the spanner. It finally gave and soon he was looking at the main detonator, its two electrical terminals and the wires that linked it to a battery and the magnetic sensor. He cut the wires and insulated them with tape. Now, unless there was a booby-trap, the mine was inert and Mould was safe. He then pulled out the detonator, the primer and the hydrostatic clock – all without issue.

At last, it was over. He lit a cigarette and looked over all the pieces he had laid out on a hessian sack on the ground. Mine disposal was no longer theory. Feeling alive and absolutely bloody marvellous, Mould gathered his tools up and walked away.

THREE
ALL THE KING'S MEDALS

SYME WAS THE last of the Australians to be blooded. Like Mould, Kessack and Reid had dispatched their first mine. Not all men selected and trained for the job were able to perform it in a live situation, and the jury was out on Syme. At around three one morning his phone rang. Birmingham had been bombed and a Blitz team was urgently needed. Syme soon found himself in a speeding car headed north.

Once there, he was taken to the first of three mines allocated to him. The police had cleared the area and set up barricades in the streets at 120 metres all around. The mine had driven through a footpath, and nearly a metre deeper into the ground, to end up resting at a slant. Outside the barricade was a disaster area. Buildings that were once homes were now like macabre dollhouse cutaways, their bricks and contents scattered along the street to be bulldozed out of the way. Birmingham was a city writhing in crisis, but as Syme stood next to his mine the world was silent and still. Like Mould, Syme struggled to overcome his acute anxiety.

Syme, too, had a seasoned officer playing nurse. At the barricades the officer advised Syme to extract the fuse remotely and wished him luck. Ever so slowly, Syme accessed the fuse and fixed a cord to it. He then retired to a dugout and pulled it free. He repeated the same action with the hydrostatic clock. These two tasks alone took him two long, intense hours. He'd been fidgeting away under the constant threat of death and failure; when he returned to the mine and saw it was safe at last he almost broke down. If he had failed, there would have been a circle of ruin to prove that he was not up to the mission. But he was, and no less than anyone else. He went and celebrated his and the neighbourhood's survival at a nearby pub. He refused the grateful locals' attempts to give him money. Their free beer, on the other hand, he accepted gladly.

The four Australians became fully-fledged RMS staff. They followed in the wake of the *Luftwaffe*, crisscrossing the country, seeing cities at their worst. On two successive nights in December 1940, Manchester suffered heavy raids. Mould's Blitz team arrived at eleven on the second night amid heavy bombing. It was Christmas Eve.

'Streets streaming with fire hoses,' he recalled in a dictated account of his war experiences. 'Everywhere there were first-aid parties working, ambulances, bombs falling down, fire flame everywhere. It was the most shocking shambles and I would never have believed the city could survive.'

Mould was allocated three mines, and at first light on Christmas Day he set off. Along the way he saw 'women clambering over rubble to get to shops to buy their little bits of poultry, or whatever they could afford, for their Christmas dinners'. Mould's gift to Manchester was three fewer mines to worry about.

Though life in London was frightening and grim, Mould managed to enjoy himself. He prefaced his recollection of good times by saying that 'under gross stress it was possible to have the greatest amount of pleasure'.

Mould's favourite watering hole was the New Yorker, a club in Park Lane that catered mainly to servicemen and opened when the pubs shut at three. Mould became a regular there not least due to the warm welcome he received from the club's manager, Margaret Massey, who would later become his wife.

'It was always a place which was bright and happy,' said Mould. 'There was seldom any drunkenness at the New Yorker. People just wanted to enjoy themselves.'

At night London could feel like a ghost town. Most people made their way home before dark to wait for the night's clamouring. One evening Mould was heading home to his digs near Sloane Square. There was snow on the ground and he had had 'a very good night out in Mayfair where I had done a good pub crawl and visits to many clubs . . . Everything was peaceful and quiet, except for the roar of the bombers and the occasional sticks of bombs dropping'.

Nearing home, Mould came across a taxi driver changing a wheel. The man refused Mould's offer of help. Mould saw that a bomb had gone off nearby, and civil defence workers were hard at work mopping up.

'Could you tell me what to do about this 'ere?' asked the cabbie, holding out a dismembered forearm.

'Good God. Where did you get that?'

'While I was mending my tyre it suddenly landed on top of the bonnet.'

Everyone was in the same boat: they had to try to cope with whatever this wretched war threw at them. And the mine disposal business was an undertaking that had a steep learning curve. You wandered through scenarios of gore, horror and ruin to deal with one mine after another. Each situation tested your wits; each mine could be luck's dead end. No one could beat luck forever, but Mould and Syme managed to keep it onside as they proceeded to shine as gifted operators.

'They were fearless chaps,' said Cashford. 'They would go where we would have to think twice and refer to our manuals. They went and did it and got away with it. They had a kind of sixth sense of, *No, I won't do that, I'll do this.* They were an example to some of us. They would go where angels would fear to go.'

The morbid fear that had threatened to overcome them on their first jobs had given way to an obsessive fascination with mines. Both Mould and Syme were intelligent and innovative, and they were prepared to back themselves. The basic mine-stripping process was by now so routine that they competed with each other to see who could extract a fuse the fastest. The more difficult problems came with mines that ended up in awkward or precarious positions, making access and dismantling a gymnastic feat of mind and body.

'Syme was the more sober one,' said Cashford. 'Mould was a happy-go-lucky sort of a fellow, except when they were on the job. They used to fight amongst themselves. They didn't always get on all palsy-walsy. Sometimes they disagreed with what the other one had done and they didn't talk for a while, and the next time you'd see them together having a pint and [being] pals.

'It was professional jealousy, you might say. They were like that. I didn't see them often, but you never saw them with a miserable face. They were always bright and cheerful.'

Their humour was certainly tested. Mould was once sent to deal with a mine that had landed next to a Shell oil refinery. If it blew, the whole refinery and its precious fuel would go with it. The problem was that the mine had sunk beyond its entire length into the estuary mud. After much thought, Mould commandeered a locomotive train, found someone to teach him how to drive it, and proceeded to drag the mine clear and neutralise it.

One time Syme couldn't access the fuse of a mine lodged in a house. He had to find a way to turn the heavy mine around silently to expose the fuse. His solution was to take the wire cable from a barrage balloon, secure one end to the mine, have the length of it run out the window, around two telegraph poles and all the way to the barricades – a total distance of 500 metres – where he fixed the other end to his staff car. He then ordered his driver to tow the cable slowly.

As he had hoped, the mine rotated. He then rendered it safe, saving an entire street of homes.

Two months after they landed in Britain, Mould and Syme were lieutenants and considered experts in their field. That's how they were referred to, even by Admiralty: the *Vernon* experts. Around *Vernon* itself, they had acquired an aura of invincibility: they were both masterful and blessed. They were revered not just for their deeds and prowess but for their character.

'They were real men,' said Cashford. 'They liked to go out with women. They liked their beer. They liked parties. They were normal men. Very nice chaps. They got on very well with practically everyone. Everyone from the same department wanted to be with them. They were such good chaps. I can't think of anything more fitting than to say that they were super fellows.

'They knew the jobs that they were doing had a short life. Several of their mates were killed. English mates. And there was a New Zealander who was very fond of them who was killed. They were very sad when any of them went. But when it came to any of the seaman, any of the team that were killed, they were the first to dip into their pockets to make some funds for the next of kin.'

Certainly, Mould and Syme had indeed cut paths of success, but their résumés were littered with colossal failures and ridiculously close shaves. For all their talent and verve, these two Australian aces lived by virtue of luck.

One event in particular was an extraordinary blend of heroism and luck. Syme was called out to a mine that lay in tidal flats. According to all Syme's experience and logic, the mine should have fired. He had to salvage the mine intact – if there was some new trick the Germans had introduced, *Vernon* needed to know. Drenched and freezing cold, he started with the detonator plate and cut the wires held inside. He had to identify the right wire to cut, but the wires were too short for him to pull clear. When he reached in with his pliers his view was blocked. Nevertheless, he closed the pliers on the chosen wire and squeezed. Instantly, there was an explosion of sparks as 180 volts shot through his body, pitching him backwards into the mud. Astounded that he was still alive and the mine was in one piece, Syme stood up, bent over the mine again and reached for the wire a second time. Again, he was electrified and thrown into the mud. On his third attempt he took another shock but succeeded in cutting the wire. He then had to take another lengthy, continual shock while he insulated the ends of the cut wire by wrapping tape around them. Syme prevailed at last, but he was burned pink. For days afterwards the outer layer of skin over his entire body peeled off. Back in the lab, no Nazi secret gizmo was found in the mine. A speck of verdigris had somehow lodged itself between the firing points to prevent the circuit from closing. All throughout Syme's ordeal the mine had been trying to fire its massive charge but had been kept at bay by a crumb.

Their near misses were terrible events, even to survive. Sometimes it was a matter of timing. Once Mould was on his way to inspect a bomb only to see it and the men surrounding it blown to pieces. He had walked behind a railway car at the critical moment. If he'd been three seconds earlier, he would have been killed too. He was on a train to London when *Vernon* was raided and his room smashed by a bomb. Another time, he had just given the all clear for a dockside mine when it went off, collapsing the dock and sending railway cars crashing into a full granary. Then there was Syme's effort to burn a mine down in Cardiff. This was a proven, though not failsafe, way to eat away the main charge and reduce the power of the blast should it go off. Shortly after Syme had walked clear of the blaze there was a massive explosion behind him. Half a brick fell from the sky that, instead of crushing his skull, merely knocked his hat off. Syme returned to the mine's location to find utter carnage. For a hundred metres around, houses were flattened outright, ruined or severely damaged. Such was the price of his 'mistake'.

Every mine disposal officer had close calls and rode their luck. One attended a mine that had landed next to St Paul's Cathedral. As he was unscrewing the ring to get at the fuse a fire engine rumbled past. Immediately, a whirring sounded from inside the mine – the clockwork fuse had come to life. The mine would blow in seventeen seconds or less and take a large chunk of St Paul's, if not the lot, with it. Instead of fleeing, Lieutenant Ronnie Smith stayed put and managed to lodge the fuse's safety pin. Another recovery officer was thrown thirty metres through the air by the shockwave of his exploding mine. He sailed towards a plate-glass window and saw the glass blow out ahead of him before he landed inside. Luck was such an absurd and fickle thing. For some, like Kessack, it didn't last. He was working on a mine in

Southport, Lancashire, when the fuse started up. He ran like hell but the blast caught him. He was awarded the George Medal posthumously.

Mould and Syme took their failures to heart. All that they prided themselves on would be suddenly and catastrophically brought into question. They were supposed to be up there with Ouvry in terms of cred around *Vernon*, yet the failures took some of the shine off – perhaps they shouldn't always be believed. But when an outcome went against their conviction, it was often a fair indication that new German technology was in play.

Mould and Syme were key agents in the knowledge war. Naval intelligence was aided by various sources, including the French Resistance and prisoners in European concentration camps forced to work the Nazi munitions factories. Yet while the intel might describe the features of a new mine, it didn't tell you how to safely dismantle it. New mines would appear on *Vernon*'s most-wanted list, and if a specimen was found only men like Mould and Syme were entrusted to secure them intact. Sometimes, though, the latest model would land in their lap.

'Quite often mines came down with new devices in them and they had the safety pin in them, as though they'd been dropped without any evil intent,' Syme said in a radio interview. 'The underground movement in France was well up to their job. We could take them to pieces without any danger at all.'

Mostly, though, secrets had to be prised out. Mould and Syme usually worked alone – *Vernon* couldn't afford to lose both of them at once – but one time they joined forces to strip a new mine the Brits called 'George'. It was a 1000-kilogram magnetic mine, but wrapped in a completely new design. Its primer and detonator were hidden under a heavy metal dome that covered the tail, and so the mine couldn't be stripped without removing this piece. Inside, however, was an ingenious booby-trap: photoelectric selenium cells. As soon as the dome was removed, light would hit the cells and they would generate a current that fired the mine. Mould and Syme were the first men to strip a live George. It was stuck down a shaft in a back alley in Stepney. Their plan was for Syme to take the strain of the loosened dome while Mould stuck paper over the two windows. They tackled it at night, but right at the moment they went to remove the dome, air raid sirens began to howl and gunfire erupted. The *Luftwaffe* had arrived. Fortunately, Mould had just managed to glue the second piece of paper in place when flares and spotlights began to light up the sky.

Syme won his first George Medal dealing with a mine that had lodged itself in the sloped retaining wall of a reservoir on Primrose Hill. It had sunk fully into the ground. Any mistake in dealing with this one and the wall would be blasted open and the neighbourhood below flooded. Syme estimated the mine's fuse to be about three and a half metres underground. Somehow he had to reach it in total silence without causing any vibrations. He thought long and hard before ruling out all options but one: he would have to dig a tunnel. So he spent the next three days doing just that, digging towards the mine with a child's (non-magnetic) wooden spade and bucket. As he disappeared deeper into the clay bank he had to get the seaman assisting him to hold the end of a long rope attached to his leg so he could be pulled back out of his tunnel when signalled. No matter how carefully Syme tended the walls of his tunnel, there was an ever-present threat of a cave-in.

On the second day of digging, he reached the mine only to discover the fuse was on the other side. Originally, he had chosen his entry point by the orientation of the mine's tailpiece, to which the parachute was attached. Unknown to Syme, though, the rear fitting had made a half rotation during impact. He had no option but to continue on and dig around the mine without so much as knocking it with his elbow. Twelve feet underground, bent foetal around a mine carrying a ton of high explosive, Syme worked until he finally reached the fuse. He cleaned the clay away, removed the fuse, then returned to the other side of the mine and removed the detonator and primer.

Mould had already earned his George Medal by the time he crossed paths with Hitler's second 'secret weapon': the acoustic mine. These weapons were fitted with a sensitive microphone. An operator could set one off with a cough. It was mid-1940 and for months now Mould had wondered if the next call-out would pit him against the latest and greatest of Germany's killing machines. No one had beaten an acoustic mine and, now that he had his chance, he was either going to be the first man to succeed or the next to die trying. Earlier, in March, he had been singled out by Captain Currey as *Vernon*'s next go-to guy for another special duty: underwater

RMS. There was a position that needed filling urgently, Currey told him. Reginald Sutherland, the man who until a week before had been pioneering underwater RMS, was 'no longer with us'. He had been blown up trying to neutralise a mine in Falmouth Harbour. The blast killed five other men who were assisting Sutherland from above. Two boats specifically built for underwater RMS duty had also been destroyed. Exactly what went wrong with Sutherland's mine was a mystery. Mould was told that he was a highly suitable candidate to replace Sutherland, if he so wished. Being singled out and sounded out were really the same thing, because Currey knew Mould was not likely to back away. Of course, Mould accepted.

He soon found himself under water off Whale Island, the site of the Gunnery School, standing on the bottom of Portsmouth Harbour in a world of darkness, learning how to dive. It was surface-fed diving, using the heavy copper helmet, an air hose, heavy boots and a thick canvas drysuit with rubber seals on the cuffs – standard diving dress. Air was pumped from above and communication between diver and surface was done by tugs on a lifeline. That Mould was to take the lead in underwater RMS was an honour, but it loomed as a poisoned chalice once the *Vernon* boffins discovered the cause of Sutherland's death. The mine he was working on was acoustic. His air bubbles, or even the rush of air circulating his suit, had proved fatal. It boggled Mould's mind to think how he could strip any kind of mine in that crazy hard-hat get-up in freezing, murky water, let alone a mine that would blast him into burley should he so much as sneeze.

Thankfully, Mould did not have to deal with his first acoustic mine under water. Located three kilometres off the coast near Humber Estuary, it was only submerged at high tide. At low tide it lay exposed on the mudflats known as Trinity Sands. By the time Mould reached it, three tides had come in, each covering the mine in five metres of water. Being submerged would have cocked the mine – it would now be alive and listening. Taking advantage of low tide, Mould, an assistant and an observer trudged out across the mud to the mine. As luck would have it, the weapon had landed in a perfect position for Mould's work – the fuse and primer faced out one side, the detonator plate the other. The question now was his method.

Proceeding in the conventional way, Mould would disable the fuse with a gag and then work on the primer. In absolute silence. The mine was all ears; a second-long audible was all it needed to blow. As he worked, Mould kept every movement to less than a second and then paused. Bit by bit he made his way to the most critical point: the removal of the primer spring. As Mould loosened the outer ring, this powerful spring would be pushing outwards. He couldn't just let it fly. From past experience he knew that it always rang out loudly and scraped against the casing as it sprang. Both he and Syme had theorised a great deal about how to tackle this problem. They had differing views, Syme arguing that a slow and sure withdrawal was the only answer. Mould, however, had resolved long before Trinity Sands that he would position himself in front of the opening, take hold of the spring and yank it out as quickly, and noiselessly, as possible. That was Mould's theory. Now he had to apply it for real.

He held tightly onto both the spring and outer ring while positioning himself directly over the fitting. In one sudden motion, he ripped his trophy towards him as though taking a hasty, awkward mark. It wasn't as clean as he had hoped. The spring cried out treacherously, but he smothered it against his body. The mine lay there, oblivious. The dumb brute was still alive and there was much more painstaking, silent work to do, but Mould had dispatched the most unpredictable hazard. He continued on, with renewed focus and sure hands to remove the primer and detonator. Finally, the mine was conquered and he could relax. He emerged from an intense, meditative trance and stood over the carcass, the first man to strip a live acoustic mine.

This feat earned Mould the George Cross. For the second time in six months George VI pinned a medal on John Stuart Mould, the first man to be awarded both the King's badges of honour.

FOUR
DAWN OF THE FROGMEN

IN MID-1941, ANOTHER Australian turned up at *Vernon*. He was a thirty-two-year-old sub-lieutenant who had wanted to deal with mines since the day he arrived at Liverpool. From his ship on the Mersey, he had watched a boat pass by and disappear into thick fog. A moment later there was a huge explosion. The boat was destroyed and all hands, some of whom may have just given him a friendly wave, were lost. The event had affected him deeply. He wasted no time offering himself to the mine disposal squad.

There wasn't much of this bloke to look at: the pint-sized newcomer appeared better suited to jockey silks than a military uniform. He stood five foot five in size four shoes, but he was lucky to be standing at all – as a boy he had contracted diphtheria. He was kept at home for treatment, as was the norm, where a yellow flag was nailed to the front fence as a public warning. When his condition deteriorated, a nurse moved into the home to relieve the boy's mother. It was to no avail. One day, fearing the worst, the nurse put a mirror to the boy's mouth. Seeing no hint of breath, she informed the mother that her son was dead. The mother grew hysterical, refusing to accept the nurse's verdict, swearing she could see the boy's eyelids move. To appease her, the nurse put the mirror to the boy's face again. This time a faint smear of mist appeared. The boy – or 'The Resurrection', as the nurse took to calling him – gradually improved, but by the time he was well he couldn't walk. A doctor advised the parents to move from their house in Broken Hill to the coast. They needed to get the boy into the sea every day and massage his legs, so they moved to a beachside suburb in Adelaide and followed the doctor's advice to the letter. It worked – the boy learned to walk again. This could well have ranked as his life's finest achievement, but it was only the start. Ahead lay the most extraordinary of military careers. To this day, Leon Verdi Goldsworthy remains the most highly decorated officer in Australian naval history.

Goldsworthy was thirty when the war broke out, and he was more than eager to serve. By 1940, he had tried to join the army, the navy and the air force, and had been rejected by all three. He was refused on two counts. The first was his height. It didn't seem to matter that years of gymnastics and wrestling had put him in fine physical shape; he was just too short. The second issue was the fact that he had hammertoes. The pinkies on both feet were permanently arched up and recoiled. For the army, hammertoe was one of those conditions that meant automatic disqualification, no ifs or buts. After failing Goldsworthy at first, the navy got back to him and told him to reapply. In March 1941, he entered the Royal Australian Naval Volunteer Reserve (RANVR) through the Yachtsmen Scheme. His record reads: 'Small toes missing, Rt and Lt feet'. Goldsworthy couldn't do anything about his height, but his deformed toes were another matter. Following the rejections, he had taken himself to hospital and had them amputated.

Goldsworthy arrived in Britain as the Blitz was ending. He joined the Land Incident Section in London, which still had its hands full dealing with unexploded ordnance all over the country. These men had acquired such prestige that trains were made available to them on demand, ready in an hour. Mould and Syme, now legends, were based at *Vernon* under the grand master Ouvry. They were still the go-to guys for 'the nasties', the new weapons that had to be retrieved intact wherever they were found, but they had both been retasked to deal with sea mines in and around their natural element: water.

Germany's mine-laying efforts had become somewhat conventional again – targeting shipping, not cities – but the rapid pace of their technological advancement never slackened. New types of Nazi moored mines were wreaking havoc, one being fitted to a delayed-action sinker that would release the mine to hull depth after minesweepers had passed over. Left unsolved, the only answer to the widespread use of this mine would be constant sweeping, an impossible task for Britain's already stretched fleet. Again, a new mine posed a dire threat to Britain's supply lines. (It was Syme who finally managed to retrieve the first sample of the sinker for examination.) On other mines the Germans added extra sinkers to the mooring line; if the mine broke free of its main sinker it would re-anchor at a shallower depth. On top of this was another problem: the vast number of mines washing ashore. During strong gales, contact mines laid by Britain, Holland, Belgium, Germany and France broke their moorings and drifted onto the shale and sand of Britain's coastline or else blew up on the rocks. Others still had been cut by sweepers but not destroyed. Tending to these wretched orphans was just the latest cause to which Mould and Syme had been enlisted.

The ending of the Blitz only made *Vernon*'s mine countermeasure efforts harder because the latest Nazi mine technology was far less likely to end up on a city street. Now it was hidden beneath the waves. To retrieve a new mine intact, the disposal officer had to take his business under water.

≈

Goldsworthy wasn't inclined to say much in his letters home to his family. Of course he couldn't bang on about his work – it was classified – but he wasn't one to bang on about anything. He did, though, mention that he was learning how to dive. This raised a few eyebrows among the Goldsworthy family. Despite all the time they had spent in the water bringing his legs back to life, no Goldsworthy had ever learned to swim. About all he wrote on the subject of diving was that they had had trouble finding a suit to fit him, that his hands would freeze under water and how painful it was when the circulation returned.

What Goldsworthy couldn't say was that he was having to use those hands to hold tools to strip mines, that those frozen fingers were his eyes when the mud and filth was too thick to see, that he had to be quiet and steady and sure-handed when there were currents pushing him against the mine or pulling him away, that there was absolutely nothing he could do but take a few last breaths if the fuse started running like some wicked little tattletale. That was what Goldsworthy meant by 'learning how to dive'. He didn't need to be able to swim. All he needed was to take the prowess he had demonstrated on land and put it to use under water.

Like Mould and Syme, Goldsworthy became absorbed in the psychological battle of mine warfare. The relationship between weapons engineers on one side and disposal officers on the other was an intimate feud. These remote enemies were drawn into one another's minds. Goldsworthy had come to mine disposal with especially good credentials. A background in electrical engineering and physics aided his comprehension of war machines. After disposing of mines in the post-Blitz clean-up, Goldsworthy was moved to *Vernon*. An even-tempered but exacting man, Goldsworthy was neat and well mannered, and he liked to see such qualities in others. He must have found Pompey very much to his liking. Like Mould and Syme before him, he was given a quick education in buoyant mines and then sent to clear 'drifters' from the beaches.

At this time, Mould was spearheading efforts to develop a diving rig specifically suited to underwater mine disposal. This was a major departure from diving tradition. Up until the Second World War, navy divers did salvage work, retrieved items dropped overboard and carried out ship repairs. They were called 'standard divers' and tackling mines was never in their job description. Diving was run by the Gunnery branch. Members would do diving as a secondary qualification, so they would have crossed guns as their right shoulder patch and a diving helmet on the cuff. Their kit – the classic Siebe Gorman suit – was practically the same as the day it was invented a century earlier. But that was about to change. The standard diving dress was too cumbersome, restrictive, noisy and magnetic for mine disposal. An alternative had to be found, and the catalyst for new ideas came blindingly to light by way of events in the Mediterranean theatre of the war.

In a series of ballsy, preposterous and ultimately triumphant raids, a bunch of elite Italian commandos turned the concept of diving on its head. On 19 September 1941, two British tankers and a cargo ship were sunk at Gibraltar. Limpet mines had been placed on their hulls by hand while they were anchored in a secure harbour. The culprits were 'human torpedoes', members of Italy's *Decima Flottiglia Mas*, the legendary 10th Assault Vehicle Flotilla. To get to the ships, the Italians had ridden torpedos that they had converted into underwater, double-seated mopeds. But these charges were no Vespas; they handled so poorly that the riders called them '*maiales*', Italian for 'pigs'. Two months later, on the night of

18 December 1941, the Italians struck a phenomenal blow in the Egyptian port of Alexandria. In a daring raid, six frogmen on three *maiales* eluded the British defensive nets and booms to sink two battleships – HMS *Queen Elizabeth* and HMS *Valiant*. This was a critical loss, but because the ships were floating just a metre off the bottom, the British were able to maintain the illusion that they were battle ready and their Mediterranean Fleet was still commandingly strong.

The dramatic exploits of Italian charioteers impacted the war in two key ways. Firstly, Churchill demanded to know what the hell had become of the X-Craft, the Royal Navy's midget submarine that had languished in the experimental phase. The neglect was redressed posthaste and two years later six X-Craft combined to make a successful attack on the *Tirpitz*, the German battleship that had spent the war tucked away in the fjords of Norway, a closeted threat that Churchill had pined to extinguish. Secondly, the breathing sets the Italians used were a revelation. They were rubber air bags made by Pirelli that fitted like airline passenger life vests. There was a breathing hose on the top and an oxygen cylinder below. The diver breathed in and out through the same hose, the exhaled air passing through a carbon dioxide filter. The scrubbed air remained in the bag to be breathed again. The diver just had to top up the oxygen content with bursts from the cylinder. This was a rebreather, a closed-circuit breathing apparatus. Not only did it conserve oxygen, it had the serendipitous benefit of not releasing any bubbles: it was perfect for covert operations.

Earlier missions by the Italians had ended in death and

failure. Their kit and torpedoes fell into enemy hands. The Brits were actually very familiar with the rebreather – it was pretty much their idea. The Pirelli model was based on 'the Amphibian', a mobile diving rig made by Siebe Gorman, an English company. The Admiralty didn't see any value in purchasing the Amphibian, and the idea of using it for offensive dive operations never occurred to them. The Italian navy thought differently and contracted Siebe Gorman to set up shop in Italy. Needless to say, Admiralty's attitude changed very quickly. They took another look at the Davis Submerged Escape Apparatus, a thirty-year-old rebreather kit made for submariners as well as other gear used for underground mine rescue and fire fighting.

Focus hardened on dive technology. The Italian jobs made everyone look at the diver as a free and mobile agent. He didn't have to be hanging off a leash and fed air by a boat and crew above. Suddenly, there was a whole new range of combat diving missions to master, each needing customised gear. To this day, the 'no-bubbles' set remains the go-to rig for infiltration and sabotage work. But there is a major issue with diving on pure oxygen: it becomes toxic at depth. Spend enough time deeper than nine metres underwater breathing pure oxygen and you will risk having convulsions. If you can't recover and surface, or at least reach a safe depth, you will die. So for covert attacks pure oxygen is great. To work on a mine that is lying deeper than nine metres, you need to breathe something more diluted.

To develop a safe underwater mine disposal rig, Mould, now a lieutenant commander, had teamed up with Siebe

Gorman, Professor J. B. S. Haldane and the Admiralty Experimental Diving Unit. The whole outfit had to be non-magnetic, but metals had to be used for the high-pressure parts. And the rig had to be silent. Ultimately, Mould came up with the Mould Mine Recovery Suit. It featured a hard hat and two-piece suit. The diver breathed from two gas cylinders that he carried on his back plus a third that was used to control his buoyancy. Even though the diver still wore heavy boots and did his work standing upright, the rig was comfortable, agile, mobile and quiet – a quantum leap from standard diving dress.

Goldsworthy assisted Mould with this vital research-and-development project. The newcomer regularly put the fruits of their labour to the test as he built an impressive catalogue of underwater disposals. He was awarded the George Medal for two jobs. The first was a parachute mine that had fallen into a half-loaded coal barge docked in Southampton. It struck with such force that it had carried through the mound of coal, through the hull and disappeared into the mud below. The scuttled barge then sank on top of it. Two years later the area needed to be dredged. The barge was removed but the mine was still there. Locating it was hard enough, but several small charges were used to clear the coal away. This made the mine highly unstable. Regardless, Goldsworthy dived on it and managed to remove the primer, but the fuse was stuck. Lieutenant Geoffrey John Cliff, another Australian, then took a drill to the keeper ring of the fuse, but to no avail. Eventually they were able to tow the mine away and detonate it.

A similar operation was carried out in Silvertown, London, where a mine was buried in mud nearly five metres below the riverbed. A concrete caisson was built on the foreshore and then a mini pier and lifting frame were constructed to hoist it directly over the mine and lower it down. At low tide, as the mud inside was dredged away, the shaft sank lower and lower until it had reached the depth of the mine. Water was kept in the shaft to keep pressure on the mine's hyrdrostatic unit so that the safety pin remained lodged. Goldsworthy then dived into a five-and-a-half-metre well full of muddy water to defuse the mine. His George Cross followed a few months later after performing a series of disposals. In claiming the scalps of regular ground mines, magnetic and acoustic mines, Goldsworthy had demonstrated not just extraordinary courage but ingenuity.

Mine warfare was insanely fertile in its own sad and contradictory way: the hothouses of invention turned out ever more odious weapons, and ordinary individuals emerged who were seemingly born to carry out the most chilling and strangest of missions. Goldsworthy before the war: employee at a neon light company who couldn't swim. Goldsworthy after: underwater mine disposal expert extraordinaire.

Soon *Vernon*'s diving program acquired another important new objective. It came in the wake of the Allied victory in the Tunisian Campaign in May 1943. By this time, planning for the invasion of Europe was already a year old and D-day itself was a year away yet, but the discovery of a cache of German mines in the Tunisian port of Bezerte pulled Mould and Goldsworthy into preparations for the greatest amphibious landing in history. The seized mines had been fitted with six-day clocks. The Germans had meant to sow them around the docks of Bezerte but ran out of time. If they had done what they intended, Bezerte would have been thrown into chaos. The harbour would have been littered with undetectable mines set to go off at any moment over a six-day period. There would have been an initial shipping casualty, or several casualties, before the port would have been completely immobilised until someone from *Vernon* could get there and figure out what the hell was going on.

Elsewhere in North Africa, Goldsworthy later wrote, 'the Germans not only mined approaches and harbours, but also planted mines under jetties, hung them over breakwaters, poked them into the machinery of slipways and concealed them in repair shops.' These developments, compounded by the fact that the Allies knew the Germans were already producing eighty-day clocks, raised serious doubts about the viability of an Allied invasion of Europe. The success of Operation Overlord – the codename for the Battle of Normandy – relied on open ports to replenish and augment the advance forces. If every captured port was found to be littered with mines on eighty-day timers, D-day could well turn out to be the most colossal failure in military history.

Not everyone held such fears following the Bezerte find. But one man certainly did – Commander C. E. Hamond – and he flagged the issue with his boss, the Director of Minesweeping. Hamond believed it was Minesweeping's duty to solve this problem. His boss agreed, and he promptly ordered Hamond to get busy finding a solution. Hamond had to discard all the prevailing minesweeping methods. Boats and machines were fine for open water, but they would not be accurate enough to scour a multi-pocketed dock, let alone one that the Germans had completely trashed. Minesweepers could never provide a guaranteed clearance to shipping. The only answer, Hamond realised, was to use *human* minesweepers. Clearance divers.

Once this idea had taken root, Hamond made a beeline for *Vernon*. He wanted another mind on the job. Actually, he wanted one mind in particular: Mould's. So he immediately set about borrowing him, and the two men nutted out a way in which every square inch of a port could be searched and cleared. Since visibility was expected to be poor, Hamond thought the divers could be guided by fixed lines or jackstays. They then refined the way the divers would search. Once a reference line was set on the sea floor, the diver could walk and search down one side of it, step over and then walk back, searching the other side. This would clear a four-metre-wide strip as much as 120 metres long. Both were satisfied with this basic system. From there, they had to find volunteers to train and form what became known as 'P Parties'. (The 'P', incidentally, didn't stand for 'port' but, oddly, 'party'. In the early stages, when it was decided there would be two parties, they were listed as P1 and P2.)

About a hundred volunteers responded to the call for 'special service'. Many had never swum, let alone entertained the idea that they would be screened as potential divers. Being told to don some weird contraption and breathe under water must have bent a few minds. Mike Connolly, a young seaman from Claygate in Surrey, found himself first cab off the rank.

'I was the first one to do a dive,' he remembered. 'I was too frightened to say no. I went down and there was a trained navy diver on the bottom. We landed in a bomb splash, up to our waist in mud. There was a great big weight on the bottom and a rope leading to the surface. This was in standard gear – the helmet. I held onto the rope because I knew that that was the way up. But after the first time I loved it.' (Connolly enjoyed it enough to make a career of diving after the war, clocking up around 50,000 dives over his lifetime, which now stands at eighty-five years.)

Three weeks after D-day on 6 June 1944, two P Parties, each consisting of around forty men, arrived at Cherbourg. The battle for the town was just about over, but the Germans had defended it for four days. In all, they had spent eighteen days carrying out a clinical demolition and sabotage job on the port. The Allies needed operational berths quickly, especially since the artificial harbours constructed for the D-day landings had been damaged by storms. The P Parties got to work.

Goldsworthy had been eager to join the P Parties but was not permitted to. His expertise was still needed for mining work – in the homeland docks, on the beaches and in the Channel. He arrived at Normandy a few days after D-day, as part of a recovery party searching for new types of mines, the nasties. When the P Parties in Cherbourg found such a mine – a K-type, nicknamed 'Katy', that was able to elude all minesweeping efforts developed for acoustic, magnetic and contact mines – Goldsworthy was sent in. This was a mine *Vernon* was very keen to get a close look at, and they entrusted Goldsworthy with its recovery. Cherbourg made for an appalling sight.

'Bridges and lock gates were crumbled masses of steel,' wrote Goldsworthy. 'Whole ships lay on their sides, effectively blocking entrances and exits. In the machine shops, lathes, drills, rollers and benders were run together in great masses of still hot metal. Barges loaded with mines were sunk alongside wharves. Trucks full of every type of ordnance lay crushed under the fallen roof of the boat train station. Train engines were toppled into the water. In the Nandonet Tunnels were strings of railway trucks . . . loaded with mines, torpedoes and every form of frightfulness.'

Goldsworthy described the Katy mine as 'fearsome'. 'To approach the mine it was necessary to swim through a hundred yards of giant weed,' he wrote. 'The water was intensely cold and the rumbles of distant underwater explosions did not add to comfort. Despite fears of diabolical booby-traps, the mine was rendered safe.'

Goldsworthy no doubt considered that to detail the finer points of his feats would be immodest. But for this action, his military record was further enhanced with the Distinguished Service Cross, and so he pipped Syme, who won a George Cross plus the George Medal and bar (the equivalent of two George Medals), as the most highly decorated Australian naval officer.

≈

On 14 August the P Parties had declared Cherbourg clear. Two weeks later, the port was operating at half capacity. This was an outstanding success for the new kids on the naval block. The P Parties had comprehensively proved their worth. Connolly was among the men who relieved the first two P Parties. They worked for six weeks before the debilitating effects of labouring on mixed gas took their toll and they were rested for two weeks. They progressed along the coastline, diving amid the 'mud of centuries' in France and into Belgium on the heels of the liberation army, which was usually fighting just a few kilometres away. Sometimes the battle ahead hadn't moved on entirely – they had to wait for Antwerp to fall. Yet when the Allies finally captured this vital Belgian port in September 1944, the Germans unleashed the heaviest rocket assault of the war. Hundreds of V1 and V2 missiles, each carrying almost a ton of high explosives, fell on Antwerp and her port. According to Connolly, the underwater shockwave from one rocket was enough to kill a diver three kilometres away if he was in a direct line of the blast. With one of these rockets hitting the city every few minutes, the P Party divers had to get on with their mission of finding and dealing with mines.

To protect them from shockwaves, they were issued with thick padded jerseys to wear under their dive suits, with guards for their privates. The divers eschewed the protection wear. 'They were too much trouble,' said Connolly. 'We just wore ordinary woollens.'

Admiralty had initially been reluctant to put its concerted support behind the P Parties. This was an entirely new and unproven naval unit, and their job spec was too suicidal for the top brass to back with gusto.

'We were given a maximum of two operations before we'd be dead,' said Connolly. 'The life expectancy according to the navy was two trips, but you never believe it's going to be you. You think it might be the next bloke, but nothing's going to happen to you. This was the attitude of everybody.' Ultimately, the P Parties spent a year carrying out their 'suicidal' work. They didn't lose a single man in operations. The only fatality was in Antwerp, where a diver was one of hundreds killed when a rocket struck a crowded cinema.

That they never lost anyone was a matter of great pride for both the men and the brains trust behind their operations: Hamond and Mould. 'As we moved up the coast we met the army mine and bomb disposal squad, and every time there were a few missing, but we never lost a P Party diver,' said Connolly. 'Not one.'

The psychological strain of diving on mines was too much for one of Connolly's party, however. He went to pieces one night while they were on leave.

'He was kneeling on his top bunk saying, "Oh, Lord God, I will not go with any more bad women, and I will stop swearing, and I won't drink anymore if I come out of this alive!" And we made a rush at him and grabbed him, put a blanket around him until a doctor came and gave him an injection. His mind was gone completely. We never saw him again. Personally, and like most of the other divers, I wasn't bothered. Because if you're sitting on a five- or ten-ton mine and it goes off, you're not going to know anything about it, so it's not going to hurt you. That was the attitude of us all. '

When the German port of Bremen was captured in April 1945, all the P Parties – five British and one Dutch – were called in to help. Two were led by Australians: Lieutenant Maurice Batterham and Lieutenant George Gosse. Batterham had assumed command of Connolly's party at Hamburg. The P Party system was for seaman divers to locate the mines, attach a buoy to them and for the officer to render them safe or else destroy them if they were in open water.

The Bremen Harbour operation was by far the P Parties' largest undertaking of the war. By the time they finished, they had searched 900,000 square metres, covering a straight-line distance of 2400 kilometres. Collectively, they had spent sixty-seven days under water. But at Bremen there was a significant individual triumph. This was where George Gosse beat the unbeatable oyster mine, the most sophisticated German mine of the war.

Gosse's party was called from Belgium to be the first to enter Bremen. While stationed at Verden until the city fell, Gosse interrogated one of the POWs, a German officer who had helped plan the demolition of the port and its facilities. He told Gosse about the oyster mine and warned him that it was impossible to sweep for and could never be rendered safe. Gosse listened intently. This was a very sophisticated unit, he was told, that was armed by the pressure of a passing ship and could then fire by way of acoustic and magnetic units. Once armed, you couldn't touch it without setting it off. The German was telling the truth: before they began retreating, the Nazis had been reluctant to use the oyster mine because they had no idea how to defuse the damn thing themselves. Gosse was impressed. This mine was on top of *Vernon*'s most wanted list; oysters had been wreaking havoc along the Continental coastline since D-day as the *Luftwaffe* was still laying them by air.

Yet another Australian volunteer reservist, Gosse had been called to *Vernon* in late 1944 after spending three years defusing drifters in Calcutta. He came to England with a strange item amongst his luggage: a Japanese mine. He thought the *Vernon* boffins might like to see one up close. Apparently, he had cleared customs in record time and then taken the mine with him by train to London. Inside, he'd replaced the main charge with cigarettes, tea, jam and other such goodies that were scarce in England. One night at the New Yorker he met and befriended Mould. The senior officer liked the cut of this newcomer's jib and promptly offered him a job with the P Parties. Gosse, an engineer, didn't hesitate. Among other things, he loved to tinker. No sooner had he been taught how to dive than he was working on ways to improve the diving set. Then he was sent to Europe. Like Mould, Syme and Goldsworthy before him, Gosse became one of those special divers entrusted to tackle the 'nasties'.

The rating who found the oyster mine reported that it was lying on the corpse of a civilian. When asked how he knew, given the extremely poor visibility, he replied, 'He must be – he's got turned-up cuffs on his trousers.'

Gosse decided to dive on the mine immediately, at night in muddy water. The torch he took with him was useless.

He had to feel his way through. Over two days he dived on the mine, taking his time to think his next moves through. It was deadly surgery using a drill and other tools he fashioned himself. After Gosse managed to extract the primer, water poured into the tube and set off the mine's detonator. There was a small explosion, but Gosse had removed the link between detonator and the main charge. Eventually, the mine was brought to the surface and Gosse continued his improvised work until the mine was completely dismantled. For good measure, he took out two more oyster mines at Bremen. Lieutenant Heath, who served under Gosse, said later, 'If Gosse hadn't found an answer to the oyster, Bremen Harbour would have been unusable.'

On 29 April 1946, a reporter from the *Adelaide Advertiser* visited Gosse at his home. Gosse had demobilised just a month earlier, having been promoted to acting lieutenant commander. The reporter wanted to know a few details about what he had done to deserve such a high decoration as the George Cross. At first, Gosse had no idea what the guy was talking about. That he had won a medal of any colour was news to him. Then he thought being honoured for doing something he enjoyed so much was amusing.

'George Gosse, George Cross,' he said. 'Sounds very much like a test of sobriety.'

FIVE
THE NEW BREED

On a cloudless winter day, a small crowd gathered at the gates of HMAS *Penguin*. A stiff breeze stole the sun's warmth and hassled the sparkling harbour. As the people filed into the hall, the divers among them might have cast an eye from Spit Bridge all the way across to Manly and recalled the countless hours they had spent in and around those waters. Diver selection days seemed like ancient history now. They had done and learned so much in the nine months since. Twelve had passed CDAT, Number 4 included, but that was just a hurdle to reaching the main goal – getting onto the clearance diving course proper and finishing it. What mattered was to get qualified, to come here on a day such as this to collect your badge of honour, and hence to the grave you could call yourself a clearance diver. From the initial twenty-three CDAT hopefuls, only nine had made it this far. For them, training was over. Clearance diving was now their profession.

The occasion called for ceremonial dress. As families and friends took their seats, the divers stood to one side. In white tally cap, striped collar and black bell-bottoms, they looked liked sailors of old. But this was 27 August 2010, and the world awaiting these young men reflected modern-day threats. Beyond the gates of *Penguin*, clearance divers manned a counterterrorism unit, living on constant stand-by. They were on board the warship HMAS *Melbourne* as specialist boarding parties, heading to the Gulf of Aden to thwart Somali pirates and al-Qaeda supply lines. They were in landlocked Afghanistan, making the lonely walk down range to deal with another Taliban IED – improvised explo-sive device. And, as ever, they were clearing ports all around the Pacific that were still saturated with unexploded mines and munitions from the Second World War.

One by one they stepped forward to receive a black, bell-shaped patch with an old-fashioned diving helmet embroidered onto it in gold thread. They also got a certificate and a medallion, but the patch was what mattered most. This was their right-arm rate that denoted their specialist quali-fication and distinguished them on sight from every other branch in the navy. It was the mark of their sub-tribe. They would be happy to have the thing sewn straight onto their skin.

The medallion was handed over by an eighty-one-year-old veteran, a man who had cherished the sub-tribe's emblem longer than just about anyone. An escalade of gold helmets fell across his blue tie. On the right breast of his jacket, another helmet decorated his name tag. Yet another was mounted on the left coat pocket, peering out from beneath a broad awning of medals. His name was Bill Fitzgerald. Back in 1955, Fitzgerald was a member of the first group of Australians to qualify as clearance divers. Not everyone saw the need for this new branch, and Fitzgerald had made its survival his personal fight. And now here he was, shaking hands with members of course number seventy-five. The old timer was a fixture at graduation day – wouldn't miss it for the world. He never looked at the kids, generations his junior, and bemoaned a loss of standards or values. He lifted to see them. He believed that, bone deep, nothing had changed. On any given day he could drop by *Penguin*, go down to the water and see everything as it should be: the procedure around the boats and dive gear efficient; the supervision spot-on. Jobs done quickly and well. No one dawdling. No one whinging. Everyone's got the zipper on their mouth, as Fitzgerald would say, pulling his fingers across his lips. Times have changed, but the character and core values of the divers have not, and that makes him feel good. It took a lot of work by Fitzgerald and his peers to hoist that helmet a yard up the sleeve, raising it from the cuff – where a secondary qualification is displayed – to the prized real estate of the upper right arm. And it took effort to keep that insignia there – a full-blown category badge, like Gunner or Submariner – and to make sure it stood for something special.

Evidence of Fitzgerald's dedication abounds at his home on Sydney's northern beaches. If he welcomed you aboard and you proceeded to ask him all about his diving days, he might be inclined to lead you 'down below', passing framed tributes to his family history and military career, and into the darkness of his garage. He mightn't bother with the light switch but grab a torch to more quickly share something with you. He would hold a brass plaque in the funnel of light, bend forward and stare at it from a foot away – the Clearance Divers' Roll of Remembrance. Fitzgerald would lock his eyes onto the rows of words heading the list of fallen comrades, and he would read them, screwy grammar and all, with an air of revelation, like they were hieroglyphics on a tomb wall. These words mean so much to him, and he believes they have the power to allow outsiders to grasp the esoteric essence of his breed:

'When called by God to report for the last time,' he would utter in a resonant voice that crackled like kindling, 'no finer reply could be given by any man to His question: "And what did you do in your life?" than to be able to reply: "I was a member of the RAN Clearance Diving Branch."'

And with that Fitzgerald would then straighten himself. 'Beautiful,' he would say with satisfaction, still looking at the plaque. Only then might he think about going for that light switch.

Over the years Fitzgerald had buried a few divers, and that Roll of Remembrance passage was his template for eulogies. 'All I do is change the name,' he said. 'Everything stays the same. It's the perfect eulogy for a clearance diver.'

Once all the certificates were handed out, two awards were announced. The first was for the dux of the course, named in honour of John Ingram, a highly respected diver who drowned on duty off Rose Bay in 1962. Every year, the shield bearing his name goes to the diver who has attained the highest standards over all the various phases of the course. From demolitions to deep, surface-fed diving to underwater tools to covert beach surveys to mine clearance to explosive ordnance disposal, recruit Number 10 James Ingram (no relation to John) was the stand-out. You could say Ingram had the advantage of starting young. He was snorkelling at age three and scuba diving at eight. He would swim alongside his father at three or four metres below, breathing from his dad's secondary regulator. After school, Ingram had studied sports science and business, so perhaps it was no surprise that he excelled in both practice and theory. Like everyone else, though, he found the course to be a steep learning curve. CDAT may have been testing but it was just ten days long. Clearance diving basic training was a thirty-week apprenticeship that was as physically taxing as CDAT, if not more at times. Additionally, with safety being paramount, they had to learn to do everything by the book. Stress levels were high, often compounded by lack of sleep, and their overloaded brains struggled to absorb a barrage of finicky step-by-step procedures. Operating in the perilous underwater environment, always buddied up with another diver, the lessons taught were tools for their own survival and that of others. Even Ingram, the star pupil, felt immense relief when the ordeal had finally come to an end.

The second award was the Gutz Effort Award, reserved for the most outstanding performer in physical training sessions.

The winner was none other than CDAT candidate Number 4: Matthew Johnson. After almost being pulled off course on day two of diver selection, he had gone on to impress at every training session. The doctor who attended to him on CDAT had warned Johnson to keep something in reserve. It seemed that advice went in one ear and out the other. Johnson can't seem to train by halves. His fierce competitiveness is too hardwired.

'I suppose I haven't really learned,' he said with a wry grin. 'No. I haven't. And I'm not going to. I try to stand out and encourage the boys. I go a hundred per cent – don't hold back. I just like to hurt myself, really.'

Before Johnson took hold of his prize, a special announcement was made. From this day onwards, the Gutz award was to be named in honour of a certain veteran who embodied the true-grit spirit of its warrant. So, Seaman CD Matthew Johnson became the first graduate to receive the rechristened prize: the Bill Fitzgerald Gutz Effort Award.

≈

In the years that followed the end of the Second World War, the British Navy sought to consolidate all the diving strands hot-housed by intense conflict. They took the knowledge banks of the underwater RMS teams, the X-Craft personnel and the P Parties – all of which had refined their diving gear to suit their particular needs – plus the trade skills of the standard diver, and proceeded to mould a new specialist they called the clearance diver. The Royal Navy formed its first clearance diving team in 1950, and the next year the Australian Navy followed suit. The RAN Clearance Diving Branch was born.

At least Australia's *commitment* to building a team was born. To get an operational unit up and running, a qualification course was needed. Recruits had to be brought up to speed, technically and physically, across a variety of skills and dive sets. By this time Mould, Syme, Goldsworthy and Gosse had all left the navy. They went and got on with their lives. Commander Mould and his wife, Margaret, in time returned to Sydney where he resumed his architecture career. Lieutenant Syme rejoined management at *The Age* in Melbourne. He later refused the offer of a knighthood, feeling it wasn't right that he should be elevated above so many others who did their RMS duty with equal selflessness. Lieutenant Commander Gosse resettled in Adelaide. A delightful eccentric, he continued to tinker away at inventions in his shed, pull fire-breathing stunts at parties and on Anzac Day swap uniforms with his cousin Jim, who had served in the army and was about a foot shorter. Lieutenant Commander Goldsworthy resumed his modest job with a neon light company in Perth, worked on his golf handicap and never drove – injuries from an underwater blast left him prone to sudden blackouts. There was, however, one man still serving who was perfect for the job of getting the clearance diving branch off the ground: Lieutenant Commander Maurice Batterham.

Batterham joined the navy in 1942, having learned electrical and mechanical engineering on General Motors' payroll.

After completing RMS training at *Cerberus*, he was sent to the war's nearest battlefront: Darwin.

Following the first and most intense raids of 19 February 1942, in which some 188 planes were used, the Japanese directed another forty-five attacks on Darwin alone in a campaign that peppered the breadth of Northern Australia and continued until November 1943. In the wake of these attacks, there was no shortage of unexploded bombs to deal with. Then there were the mines. Batterham had arrived in Darwin on the heels of Lieutenant C. G. Croft, the first man to render Japanese mines safe in Australian waters. In all, Croft dealt with twenty-one mines found along the north-west coast. Sometimes he and his team had to walk for days to reach a drifter lodged in a mangrove swamp infested with sandflies, mosquitoes and crocodiles. Croft went on to serve in Britain.

Batterham certainly had his hands full in Darwin, disposing of more than a hundred bombs and mines. One bomb crashed through the top of an oil storage tank and continued downward through two metres of sludge, through the bottom of the tank and into the sand beneath. In pitch black, Batterham dived through the slimy muck, felt his way through the hole, found the bomb and removed its fuse. A year later, he was diving in the icy waters of northern Europe, disarming German mines by feel in head-high mud.

At the end of the war, a massive clean-up job remained in the Pacific. Thousands of mines had been laid along the Great Barrier Reef. In New Guinea and the Solomon Islands vast amounts of Japanese and American ordnance had to be removed to allow life and commerce to get back to normal. A preliminary assessment of Japanese stockpiles and minefields from Indonesia to New Guinea was made by Croft, by now a lieutenant commander, who had returned from the UK with a George Medal and bar to his name. In Rabaul, Croft and Batterham joined forces to spearhead the clearance job, with Japanese POWs used for labour on land and pump hands at sea. Batterham then returned to Australia, where he became Assistant Director of Underwater Weapons.

Before the job of forming an Australian clearance diving team landed on Batterham's desk, all navy diving matters, along with bomb and mine disposal work and demolitions, were handled by the Torpedo and Anti-Submarine Branch, which had taken over from Gunnery. HMAS *Rushcutter*, the torpedomen's base at Rushcutters Bay, Sydney, had become home of the standard divers and of the dive school that trained and qualified them. Several standard divers had been put through bomb and mine disposal courses and, given the abundance of mop-up work left to do in New Guinea and elsewhere, they had begun to see the sense in building a permanent, port-clearance capability. Naturally, that would be their job because for anything that needed doing diving-wise, the standard diver was your man. This, however, was no longer the view from up top.

When the news broke that an entirely new clearance diving team was to be formed, and that this squad of 'specialist' divers was to be forged from a bunch of volunteers – who could trundle in from any old corner of the navy – and that this mob was going to be granted the licence to run its own show, at *Rushcutter* to boot, right under the noses of the mighty standard divers, the hard-hat men could only soothe their bruised egos with the relish that they would get to watch these clowns fail. When the first batch of volunteers arrived at *Rushcutter* for the first clearance diving course, the standard divers would not be throwing them a welcome party.

The signal calling for volunteers had gone out in January 1955. This was no back-straightening pitch that cocked a stern eye and gripped your heartstrings, just a bland communiqué, a simple telex. 'Volunteers required. First clearance diving course. No experience necessary. Submit your name and wait to be called in to take a test dive.' What caught Jake Linton's eye was the money: tuppence a minute. He wasted no time applying.

Linton was a nineteen-year-old able seaman whose life had been torn apart. His first-born, a boy, had died at ten weeks and his wife was still recovering in hospital. He worked as a sentry at the Garden Island naval headquarters by day and then would head over to the Rocks to moonlight at Playfairs meat company, lugging meat around a vast freezer. Still, he was not earning enough to pay the medical bills and bring his wife home. *Tuppence a minute.* He did the sums. In three hours' diving he could earn what he made in a night at Playfairs: thirty shillings. This was excellent pay. Here was an opportunity for him to get by on just one job. And if you dived below fifty-five metres it was ten pence a minute. Linton soon found himself under water at Rushcutters Bay doing his test dive. Around 300 sailors had applied, not a standard diver among them. Eighteen were accepted.

Why so many came forward may have had something to do with the public fascination with one of the most intriguing products of the war: frogmen. In post-war Australia, the underwater world had become a popular domain. Flippers and goggles were de rigueur at the beach. The growth of spearfishing was so dramatic that trawlermen were crying foul. But for all the fun and frivolity of the mask and snorkel, a powerful mystique surrounded navy combat frogmen. Newspapers ran eye-popping war stories – *Secret Until Now!* – about human minesweepers and underwater knife fights. In their black suits and masks, the divers made an awful, riveting sight, so horrifically sci-fi as to be labelled 'grotesque', as if they had just emerged from some primordial swamp. Otherwise they were marvellous wonderbeasts – half man, half fish – that had more acrobatic pep than a seal and a big knife to boot. There was even a feature film called *The Frogmen* (1951), based on the US Underwater Demolition Teams that had blasted clear landing lanes for amphibious attacks on Japanese island strongholds in the Pacific. Batterham was invited to speak at screenings. Then there were the diving exhibitions the Australian navy would put on for Trafalgar Day – back when they heartily embraced all things Royal Navy, including the tradition of celebrating Nelson's great victory – where divers would demonstrate to the public (no cameras allowed) how they repaired and sabotaged ships. Yet for all this interest and intrigue, many volunteers would have simply been eyeing the cash or else wanting to flee their ship to be free of a despised superior.

The course was very much Batterham's baby, but once it was up and running he was confident enough to let go of the reins. Based at Naval Office in Melbourne, he visited the men weekly. He was a tall gent with a pipe ever planted in his mouth and he befriended men of all rank. He left the running of the course to Commissioned Gunner Ron Hillen, the lightweight boxing champion of the fleet. Hillen was a deep diver who had qualified as a clearance diving officer in the UK. The day-to-day program was handled by Lieutenant Ron Titcombe, a sharp administrator and qualified diver who had a strained relationship with the men under his command. He was the runt put in charge of the litter, and he tended to overcompensate. His real strength was the work he put in behind the scenes for the divers and the branch: some regarded him as a visionary. Titcombe's shortcomings, though, left room for the stronger personalities among the divers to take charge. Ultimately this worked in the divers' favour because they had a battle on their hands from the start.

The eighteen newcomers and their supervisors came and went via *Rushcutter*, where they would take a launch out to their base proper, HMAS *Porpoise*. This so-called base was a concrete ammunition lighter – a flat-decked barge built to transfer ordnance from depot to ship – moored off Clarke Island. They got their stores from navy headquarters at Garden Island across the bay. There were a couple of sheds on the lighter that served as accommodation and storage, and three men maintained a duty watch every night while the others went home to their families or stayed in their digs at

Rushcutter. While they were subject to navy rules and saluted whomever needed saluting around *Rushcutter*, they had no duties there and completely ran their own show. The standard divers had no control over them whatsoever.

'There was no fisticuffs,' remembered Linton, 'just eyeballing. They were on one side of the street and we were on the other. I think they really did expect that we would fail, that none of us would qualify to handle the equipment.'

From the outset, the rigours of diving made a high level of physical fitness paramount. The six-month course had started mid-autumn and would run all through winter. Every morning at seven thirty they donned their fins and jumped into the water for a three- or five-kilometre morning swim. No wetsuits, just overalls. As the water got colder they took to wearing two-jumper long johns: one as a top and the other as pants, putting their legs though the sleeves and sewing up the neck. They would fin on their backs across the harbour and return, or continue over to Garden Island. In time they learned to wear their overalls inside out because the pockets dragged. Still, it felt like they were swimming with anchors, so they cut holes in the pockets.

'It's not cold!' they would declare, but it took them a long while to recover from an hour's swim mid-winter, having to shove their hands into a bucket of warm water to get their fingers moving again. 'There are no sharks!' was another catchcry. There were sharks, all right, but Sydney Harbour was teaming with sea life and the sharks had plenty of fish to eat. They were bitten and stung plenty of times, but by what exactly usually remained a mystery. After the morning swim and PT, the group would boat over to *Porpoise* for their course instruction.

The standard divers must have been amused to see this bunch of yoyos toing and froing, jumping off the wharf, duck-diving and coming up with a handful of mud to show they had hit bottom on a breath-hold, up on land doing push-ups and squats and what-the-hell-ever else. In and out of the water like bloody startled seals, they were. In a way, these wallies brightened up the joint, tickled the funny bone. Yet there wasn't just mirth in the old guards' eyes; there was jaundice. And they were not about to stand by idly while these ring-ins swanned around all over their turf, which was not just the very concept of navy diving but the gear, the supplies and the refills provided by navy, the naval docks and bases, and the harbour and seven seas beyond, for that matter. Even though this clearance diving business was a Navy Board initiative, it was by no means a *fait accompli*. Whether or not it survived, and in what form, remained to be seen. Batterham had a hard time getting his men access to various areas to conduct exercises. Taking up the fight on the ground was Bill Fitzgerald, a young man not inclined to take a backward step. Ultimately, the true believers had to be the divers themselves.

'You fought hard to become a clearance diver,' recalled Fitzgerald. 'We did it really hard.'

Compared to the other volunteers, Fitzgerald was old. He was all of twenty-four, a petty officer, a veteran of the Korean War and bomb disposal missions in New Guinea. He had been a sonar operator in the torpedo branch and had tried to get qualified as a standard diver in 1949 but was barred by his direct officer. He then had to push to get onto the clearance diving course and was made a special over-age case because he was so keen. Fitzgerald was not just doing the course, he also taught in areas he was qualified in, such as bomb and mine disposal and demolitions – skills he had learned from Croft and applied in New Guinea. Most importantly, he had grown up on navy bases and through his father had met many high-ranking officers. He knew exactly where he stood and he did so firmly.

'The only thing that kept us up and running and stopped us from being overpowered by the old guard was Fitz's personality,' said Linton. 'He was able to keep the standard divers at bay. If he hadn't have been there the outcome might have been different. Because of his seniority and strength of character, although he was a member of the course just like the rest of us, he used to be the mother hen and keep us away from the standard divers who wanted us to fail.'

The would-be clearance divers were on a mission. They were determined to prove themselves and credit the faith Batterham had placed in them. They quickly came to see themselves as the new breed – an elite, highly mobile, multi-skilled diving unit. They pulled together immediately, a team from day one.

SIX
LIFE ON THE EDGE

THE DAYS FOR the *Porpoise* crew were full. In Sydney Harbour they learned how to search for underwater mines and render them safe. Out at the army's Holsworthy artillery range, they practised their disposal skills on unexploded bombs. British commandos taught them rappelling and beach reconnaissance. Ship attack, considered very glamorous after the war, was a must. Underwater ship repair was also on the curriculum. Demolition classes were centred on a sunken wreck off Chowder Bay. The brick-shuddering blasts didn't win them too many friends in the shoreline neighbourhoods, but they did deliver plenty of fish. The blast catch became fare for the Friday afternoon barbecues they held. Elsewhere in the clean and bountiful harbour, a harvest of oysters, mussels and lobsters could be added to the menu. The testing life certainly had its perks.

Diving was, of course, their main activity. If they weren't out on a dive they were preparing for one. Most days they spent four hours under water and conducted at least one night dive a week. They readied their own rigs and filled their own cylinders using a mechanical pump. Then it was into the water in shifts: one team laying a dummy minefield and then another 'swimming string', doing jackstay searches, to find and clear them. However, one drill in particular was paramount: the oxygen swim.

Swimming on pure oxygen was always an inherently dangerous task, so mastering the rebreather was essential. From day one the divers had to learn how to follow a given compass bearing while maintaining a safe depth of no more than eight metres. Having no reliable depth gauges, they had to do this by sight, and it was a pretty rough guide: if they couldn't see the shimmer of the surface, they knew they were too deep. The air bag was also the diver's buoyancy control vest. He had to balance how much gas he let into the bag against how much he consumed by breathing. This was particularly hard at shallow depths when trying to stay covert and not break the surface. All up, oxygen swims honed a diver's navigational skills, depth maintenance and diving discipline.

In September 1955, eleven volunteers qualified as clearance divers. Australia had its first clearance diving team. From the eighteen starters, six had withdrawn during the course and one had deserted the navy altogether. Individually, every diver was proud to pass, but the success of the unit had become their collective cause. They desperately wanted to stick it up anyone who ever doubted them. That same year, the Siebe Gorman hard-hat rig was removed from all Australian ships. The copper helmet and canvas suit ensemble was consigned to the museum. Standard diving itself would soon follow.

Navy diving's generation-next was on its feet. Working out in the open on Clarke Island, they operated in full view of the Fleet Commander's office at Garden Island and the general public, at least waterside residents and harbourgoers. Wider knowledge of who they were and what they did remained limited. The sight of specialist divers setting up camp in the middle of Sydney Harbour piqued the interest of the press. Despite Batterham being tight-lipped about his 'frogman school' – the navy wanted the nitty-gritty of their affairs kept under wraps – a few admiring write-ups appeared. But what really mattered to the divers at this point was their internal validation and establishing an indispensable role for themselves within the navy – a feat no amount of column inches could achieve.

One sure way to win a captain's respect is to sink his ship, right under his nose. It won't be a warm-and-fuzzy kind of respect, but it will be won nonetheless. When the clearance divers were given any opportunity to conduct 'attacks' on fleet ships, they made the most of it. Ship attacks were 'operation awkward' exercises designed primarily to test and tighten the defensive regimen of the ship's crew, so the divers' success had to come at the expense of the crew's pride.

Whenever a ship attack was planned, a date was set and the ship's crew was put on full alert. They knew that at some stage during the night the clearance divers would be coming to lay dummy limpet mines on the hull. The sailors would have their underwater lights on, spotters at all points and a patrol boat in the water. The standard defence tactic of dropping explosives overboard was, of course, not allowed.

The divers staked everything on these raids. Typically they would approach the target ship at Garden Island from three points and, to their credit, they were always able to lay their mines and were seldom caught. These were chastening defeats for the ship's crew, particularly the standard divers onboard who had to search the hull to confirm the mines had been attached. The navy brass was impressed, though. The new breed's reputation was building.

Following the successful graduation of the first clearance divers, the navy cut the standard diving qualification courses altogether. The ranks of the hard-hats began to migrate over to the new branch. Most assumed their transition would be a mere formality, but many failed to make the cut. That said, the clearance diving branch was particularly blessed to have two who did: Raymond Foord and Leo Brennan. These two men became so thoroughly admired that their better values became those of the branch itself. Foord's passion for bomb and mine disposal helped enshrine the craft as the divers' core value, while Brennan was the amiable, quiet achiever, the ultimate can-do operator. So, while effectively dancing on standard diving's grave, clearance diving did well to inherit a heavy dose of hard-hat spirit.

The six-month course was held every year and soon gained widespread notoriety for its toughness and high failure rate.

Many eager young men saw themselves as divers, but when asked to keep going – and going alone – under water, when it was pitch black and stone cold, many reconsidered. They were never kicked off course; they had to walk away of their own accord. This ensured that a supervisor didn't reject a potentially excellent diver who was merely exhausted, cold and wondering whether he should give up. You just never knew if and when the student would find his second, third or fourth wind.

Every course was an endurance test that ran from April through to October. Wetsuits only started to appear around 1960, but they did have drysuits. These were fully sealed rubber suits that you could wear a layer of clothing underneath. Still, they were not exactly toasty. The water temperature in the harbour through the year varied about degrees (about fourteen to twenty-three degrees Celsius), but the water in the graving docks of Garden Island could get much colder. Like in backyard swimming pools, the water temperature in that environment would get close to the ambient temperature. To dive a dock on a Monday morning in winter felt like a dip in the Arctic.

'I can assure you,' said Linton, 'when wetsuits were invented they were prized acquisitions.'

Each year more eager candidates arrived. For many, though, the Friday seafood barbie and beers was no compensation for the discomfort, stress and pressure of the preceding week, spending so many hours in the water you might even forget you couldn't breathe the stuff. Relentless taskings from instructors who were indifferent to your pain and fatigue, who gave you nothing when even a single encouraging nod would have lifted your spirits. The emotional distance of authority, the silent water, the damned cold and the mental anguish all pushed an individual towards a kind of solitary confinement, a morose headspace in which fears could fester into demons. Fit, strong and tough men stepped away from the course and returned to their former posting. Many others simply failed. All up, it was usual for a third of the class to fail – sometimes two-thirds. The navy's top brass had not known anything like it – why were so many seemingly eligible candidates being rejected? They sent a psychologist to see if Fitzgerald was driving these would-be divers too hard. The shrink reported that indeed he was, and Fitzgerald was told to ease up. The changes were moderate, but Fitzgerald had no time for this kind of touchy-feely interference. He believed it would cost lives.

'Bill was held in high esteem,' said Linton, 'and I don't think he was any harder than anybody else. Everybody who completed the course was proud of the fact that they had met the requirements. It was a feather in your cap. And if you had been trained under someone who was more difficult than someone else, then that was even better. I saw Fitz as a bloke who wanted all his people to survive.

'When I was instructing I had a high failure rate. Everyone did. The one thing that was always in your mind was, *If I qualify this bloke, am I happy to have him as my dive partner? Am I happy to have him holding onto my lifeline, looking after me?* And most importantly, *has he got the mental and physical aptitude, fortitude, to do it?* The product Bill was trying to turn out, what I was trying to turn out, was someone who was not only competent but confident in himself, and that was something you could only ever learn by pushing them to the limits.'

During the latter stage of the course the students would turn up at *Rushcutter* expecting the usual challenges. By now they would have looked you in the eye and told you that they had given their absolute bloody all. But on this day the navy was determined to find out exactly what 'their all' really amounted to. They were told to get to work – and they were told to keep working until they could not work anymore.

That this order was to be taken literally took a while to sink in. Eventually, as the hours mounted up, it did. The men found themselves working the longest, hardest shift of their lives. For two days they kept at it in constant rotation – diving, surfacing, charging the cylinders, preparing the gear, testing it, diving again. Four in the water at a time – morning, noon and night. The pressure stayed on all the while; only the requirements eased off as heavy fatigue began to take its toll. Each man had to decide for himself when to stop. It was over by day three. The result? Everyone else knew your limits and you knew theirs. You understood just how much faith you could put in each and every bloke.

Year by year the divers went from strength to strength. They made themselves so useful to navy that soon every ship was issued a pair. A real landmark was when they discovered a row of live depth charges lying across Rushcutters Bay. These had been dropped into the water in 1942, when one of the Japanese midget submarines was being hunted around

Sydney Harbour like a rat under a rug. It was the only one of three subs deployed that was able to attack, and as she approached Garden Island the pilot had a hard time keeping her submerged. Spotted by USS *Chicago*, she was fired upon and peppered with depth charges. The shells missed and the charges failed to detonate. The midget sub rounded to the north side of the harbour, turned and fired at the *Chicago*. The torpedo missed its target, passed under a Dutch submarine and struck HMAS *Kuttabul*, an accommodation barge, killing twenty-one Australian sailors.

The midget sub and her crew of two disappeared and were never seen again. The reason the depth charges hadn't done their job was because they were set to go off at a depth of twenty-five metres, and landed in ten. These were powerful pieces of ordnance, and their safe removal was no mean feat for the young team. Once the job was done, though, the divers felt they were at last truly accepted within navy.

In the thick of the 1958 British winter, two Australian clearance divers found themselves lumped with an unenviable task: they had to see how long they could stand the icy waters of Portsmouth Harbour. The Royal Navy scientists wanted to develop a diving suit that extended operational time in brutally cold conditions, and a team from the Admiralty Experimental Diving Unit became their guinea pigs. In charge was Phil Hawke, who had just completed the Royal Navy's clearance diving course, becoming the first Australian officer to qualify as a clearance diver. Serving under Hawke were four British seamen and the Australian petty officer Foord, who had spent seven years as a standard diver before crossing over to the new guard. In 1954, he played the lead role in the rescue of twenty-odd young sailors whose boat capsized in Port Phillip Bay as it approached Foord's ship, HMAS *Vengeance*. The men were struggling to stay afloat in their full dress uniforms, and Foord dived overboard to help them reach and hold onto their overturned boat. He thought he had them all but after a headcount on *Vengeance* it was realised that two had drowned. In 1955 he was awarded the British Empire Medal for his actions. That same year, while the first CD course was being run in Sydney, he was sent to England to undertake the Royal Navy version. He'd spent a good deal of time afterwards working on mine disposal before eventually joining Hawke's team. Working together for the first time, the two men enjoyed a good rapport, and soon enough they would be teaming up in Sydney to change the shape of clearance diving back home.

Hawke had volunteered for the branch in 1955. During a time when promotion within the Australian navy progressed at a glacial pace, most thought Hawke was crazy to deviate from the traditional, ship-focussed career path. But the young officer saw opportunity in the small, unproven diving outfit. The fact was, he was enamoured with the diving stories that were still emerging from the war. He was particularly inspired by the P Parties and the exploits of Buster Crabb, the legendary British diver who opposed the Italian frogmen at Gibraltar and, in the very harbour in which Hawke was now testing, would go missing a year later after being sent to spy on a visiting Russian cruiser's propeller. Hawke was told to report to the diving school at Rushcutters Bay for a basic diving assessment and found himself under the tough but fair supervision of Bill Fitzgerald.

'To see whether I could handle it or not, he put me under water in a suit called a "clammy death",' said Hawke. This was a rubber suit that was always wet inside from leaks, sweat and urine. It stuck to the skin, ripped body hair out and pinched flesh wherever it could, the crotch being a prime target. Sometimes divers took to writhing on the seabed in an attempt to free trapped skin. Hawke donned his hard-hat and entered the water, breathing air fed by hookah. This was Hawke's one and only litmus test – Fitzgerald could pass or fail the young officer at his own discretion. Hawke found himself under water long enough to be slightly concerned that he had been forgotten. He killed time by walking around the bottom of the bay until he was summoned. Eventually, by a tug of the line, Fitzgerald called him to the surface. Hawke had been down there for three hours. Fitzgerald passed him.

There was no way Foord, who had been known as Dixie all his life, was going to spend that long freezing his cods off in Portsmouth Harbour. The British divers could have their record of ninety minutes. 'Dixie would surface and say, "Fuck it. I'm not doing this anymore!"' said Hawke.

After the war, British clearance diving was focussed on pushing the boundaries of endurance and deep diving, as well as exploring new ways to search for mines. Only a month of Hawke's half-year course was devoted to bomb and

mine disposal, and underwater mine disposal was not covered at all. Foord developed a passion for bomb and mine
disposal, and when he returned to Australia he made sure
that it remained the focus of the branch. As one of the lead
instructors during the 50s and 60s, and the senior non-
commissioned officer running the bomb disposal schools,
he drove home the fact that rendering bombs and mines safe
was the fundamental raison d'etre of the clearance diver.

'It set the clearance diving branch on the path it has followed ever since,' said Hawke. 'The diving is simply the
means to get down to the mine.'

When Hawke was running the dive school, Foord
impressed him immensely. At the time, the division between
officer and sailor was a strict class system: the gentry gave
the orders and the working class said 'aye'. Hawke had been
in naval college since the age of thirteen and didn't meet
one sailor until he graduated at eighteen. Like many of his
peers, he was raised to consider England home. No Australian sailor did, and Dixie Foord was as Australian as they
come. Born in outback Western Australia, he had an accent
as broad as a Bradman's bat, and no amount of time spent
with the Royal Navy was going to trim it. He never wanted to
be an officer. This was not some kind of inverted snobbery, it
was just that Foord knew what he was good at, and that was
working closely with the sailors as a boss and mentor. One
day Hawke called Foord in to sound him out on an idea, and
it was a meeting that more or less led to the class division
being removed from the clearance diving branch hierarchy.

Hawke had recently been on a multi-national exercise in

Asia. As usual, the officers and sailors were segregated when it came to where they slept and what they ate. They were a divided team. There was a group of Australian Special Air Service Regiment troopers there, and Hawke noticed they did everything together. He returned home determined to make the branch more of a unit from head to toe. He told Foord that their small outfit would be far better off if they dispensed with a few divisive traditions. What they needed to do was forge a culture in which rank was respected but everything was shared and needs were equal. You could say Foord was in favour.

'I've been waiting for someone to say that for years,' he told Hawke. And Foord took up the task wholeheartedly. He told officer and sailor, as individuals and in groups, that this was the way things were going to be. They went on exercises where everyone worked together. They were all part of the same team. Generally speaking, it went down well. Everyone would dive one night a week, and then it was down to the Golden Sheath Hotel in Double Bay for a few beers. Up until then, officers and sailors never mixed socially apart from at the annual ball. The branch began to have more frequent social events, and on one occasion Foord stepped up to offer Hawke a gentle reminder.

'Sir?'

'Yes?'

'You're not mixing.'

'Sorry, Dixie.' With that, Hawke promptly got to mingling. While Foord would have stressed the importance of staying calm during bomb and mine disposal, he once inadvertently gave a practical demonstration of keeping one's cool. The team was up at Port Stephens, where they used to train. With no time to wet a line, they would fish by tossing plastic explosives into the water from their forty-foot work boat. On this occasion, Foord lit the fuse of some 'black expanding bait' and went to throw it overboard, but the explosives slipped out of his hand. Foord was up the front of the vessel while the rest of the team were aft with Hawke at the wheel. These men knew their explosives, and this charge was big enough to kill or main them all. Sensibly, they dived over the side. Hawke stayed put. Foord kicked the bomb, but it caught the guardrail and bounced back into the boat. So he stepped over, picked it up and threw it clear.

'Had it exploded, he certainly would have been killed – and I probably would have been also,' said Hawke. 'And if he and I had gone over the side, I would have been court-martialled, and he probably would have been too. He maintained calm under very real pressure. I bought Dixie a beer that night and told him how well I thought he'd done, but the sailors spread the word right throughout the branch. By the time we got back to *Rushcutter*, two or three days later, almost everyone knew.'

≈

There was an odd yet natural contradiction in clearance diving culture: their methodical systems could be undermined by arrogance. Young men were being asked to risk their lives, and they often did so with a tragic sense of invincibility.

Perhaps it should come as no surprise that this would have fatal consequences.

The need to be super fit and switched on was well understood. Human beings weren't meant to be under water for any longer than a breath-hold. The equipment allowed you to keep breathing in a hostile environment. If it failed and you couldn't reach the surface, you would die. You were the captain of your own vessel and you could abort anytime you wanted. If you started having trouble, you just had to get the hell out of there and surface. All the divers had this drummed into them. So many facets of their education – procedures they had studied, been tested on and had made second nature – were directly or indirectly safety measures. But none of the divers ever thought their particularly hazardous job might kill them. Any reference to death was only fit to be acknowledged by way of black humour. There was a well-known typo in the divers' manual. A symptom of oxygen poisoning, it read, was a twitching of the 'plis', instead of 'lips'. 'Twitching of the plis' became a phrase the divers tossed around to get a laugh.

If they wore the inherent dangers of their job lightly it was because they were so highly drilled, competent and confident. It just so happened that what they did to earn a crust was occupy a frontier post. They were at the vanguard of modern diving and getting by on a shoestring. This was no high-and-mighty mission backed by blank navy cheques. No matter how many write-ups they got in *Pix* or the *Post*, the clearance divers were more faceless guinea pigs than pride-of-the-nation poster boys. They were pushing their luck in a dangerous field and, somewhere behind their collegial shtick of jokes, grilled fish, tinnies and bulletproof bravado, they knew it. *A bloke could get killed doing this job. But that bloke ain't me.*

Tom Aldridge was the first. It was 1959 and he was among a group of divers staying down at the Pittwater Annex. Aldridge set off on his own to catch a few blackfish that lurked beneath the firing shed at the end of the wharf. He donned an oxygen set, grabbed a hand spear, jumped into the water and sank six metres or so. Shortly afterwards he lost consciousness. It would appear he suffered a shallow-water blackout, a response that can happen to anyone who suddenly goes from breathing air to pure oxygen and immediately enters a pressurised environment. The rapid change of both oxygen content in the blood and the pressure under which it is delivered can be too much for the brain to deal with, and it shuts down. Like fainting, the shallow-water blackout should be a short-lived and ultimately harmless malady. But once unconscious, Aldridge lost his mouthpiece and drowned. If he had been wearing the regulation rig, where the mouthpiece was fixed onto the mask, he would still have been able to breathe after he had passed out. Without company, there was no one to save him.

Not one diver took Aldridge for a fool. Each of them knew in his heart that at times they didn't follow the letter of the regulations book or take all the routine precautions, and they didn't push navy to buy them the best gear. They made do with, and even modified, the equipment they were given. They were backyard tinkerers who chipped away at a technological frontier. Across the world, modern diving was a work in progress. Theirs was a risky business and sometimes things went wrong. Following Aldridge's death it became mandatory for all divers to breathe from their oxygen set for a minute before entering the water. Other than that, it was as you were.

In October 1961, Kel Creasy died in Jervis Bay. Creasy was a stand-out diver. He was known to throw down a hundred push-ups on each hand, then a third hundred using both. He never blotted his copybook and was a likeable guy. He died testing a new mine-searching method where an underwater sled manned by a diver would allow a visual scan of the seabed. On a clear, calm morning, Creasy was twenty-five metres down 'riding the bull' when the boat towing the sled began to play up. The boat stopped, so Creasy surfaced and waited. Like many divers, he was always mindful of conserving gas – filling your own tanks by pump was backbreaking work – so he turned his cylinders off and began to breathe surface air. The problem on the boat took a while to resolve and Creasy, weighed down by his heavy gear, tired himself out staying afloat. He was seen working away at his breathing rig before sinking. By the time another diver reached him he was lying dead on the sea floor.

John Ingram was another cream-of-the-crop diver, yet he drowned in about ten metres of water doing a jackstay search off Shark Island in Sydney Harbour. This beggared belief, hardly any less so than if Ingram had drowned in a backyard wading pool. Exactly what happened will never be known, but Ingram's death was a strident reminder that luck's patience was finite. All the divers were accustomed to taking calculated risks for the sake of expediency, and Ingram working away on pure oxygen at borderline depth was the kind of dangerous flirtation that was routine. He was neither a maverick nor a braggart, but if you told Ingram you had swum 1500 metres in ten minutes he would go and do it in eight, and have you know so. That was his nature. On this fatal day, he just may have overstepped the limits of his capabilities. It seems he got into trouble, tried to surface but could not – no fins, heavy boots – and drowned.

Ingram's death dealt another severe blow to the clearance diving brotherhood. And it made them reassess their procedures, again, and ponder their own mortality. No doubt they did the same in August 1967, when Jeff Hales and John Hislop died carrying out a covert ship attack, by definition an exercise carried out under the cover of darkness, in Jervis Bay. While one maintained their bearing by compass, the other kept depth by eye. They strayed too deep, suffered oxygen toxicity, sank to the bottom and died. With every diving death, the men grieved and buried their mate. They did not seek to apportion blame, but were coldly reminded of their own good fortune. How many times had they strayed below the regulation eight metres on oxygen? Too many to count. Yet they were alive and Hales and Hislop were dead. The precariousness of their vocation added something exquisite to their existence, something that office johnnies could never know: the vitality of holding your own life in your own hands. They took it to heart that they had earned the right to be entrusted with such a weighty responsibility – they were trained, tested and approved by way of rigorous examination. They were bloody clearance divers. RIP Aldridge, Creasy, Ingram, Hales and Hislop and those who followed, fantastic bastards all and never to be forgotten, but it was on with the show. And soon the living returned to pitting their skill against fate, courting death here and there, trading known risk for practical expediency. It was just the way you did things.

Deeper than the job spec and pride burned a fierce competitiveness, a male-group dynamic as old as loin cloth. That each diver was alpha-male material only upped the ante. Throw a few together and, no matter how well they bonded, each and every one would aim to do more, to carry more, to never fall behind. It is precisely this kind of atavistic, tribal vibe that the military – or a football club, for that matter – seeks to harness from young men. And nothing beats a difficult mission to get this energy channelled into a common cause. In early 1961, Maurice Batterham saw a chance to put the worth of his divers on the line, and he grabbed it with both hands.

The Snowy Mountains Hydro-electric Authority (SMA), which presided over the monumental hydro-electric network that had been under construction since 1948, had a major problem. One of the dams had filled up earlier than expected. It was the Eucumbene Dam, which was essentially a massive rock and clay rampart built across a valley. It held back nine times the volume of Sydney Harbour and drained like a sink. The water ran out of a horizontal tunnel cut through the bottom of the wall before being pitched downwards into a turbine. The water had to be filtered or else large pieces of debris would jam the tunnel or career down and smash the turbines to bits. For this purpose, there was a sixty-seven-metre-high straining tower – a vertical sieve, in effect. The water entered the tower and poured out the bottom through two twenty-ton concrete swing doors and into the tunnel. Whenever the doors or tunnel needed to be inspected, a few steel beams were slotted in front, one on top of the other like a log-cabin wall, to seal up the dam-side entrance. Problem was, the SMA engineers had tried to inspect the tunnel but couldn't. They had dropped all these steel 'stop logs' into place, but there was still a metre-high torrent of water rushing through the tunnel. Someone had to dive down and see why these stop logs weren't shutting off the water properly. However, the dam was now full and the top of the tower was sixteen metres under water. To check the stop logs at the bottom, a diver would have to go to a depth of eighty-three metres in extremely cold, dark water. A French dive company quoted a million pounds up front and another million once they were done, irrespective of success. That kind of money was crazy talk, so the SMA approached the navy. Not long afterwards, Batterham was briefing his boys about a job.

Batterham must have had some reservations. To operate at that depth, a diver needed to be breathing helox (a helium/oxygen mixture), but the SMA, navy and government were all unwilling to spend the thousands of pounds needed to import helium from Canada. Because no one could say how long the job would take, the spectre of a financial blowout was very real, and that worried the SMA especially. Air was the cheap option, and the most dangerous one. As the navy knew full well, by their own rules and regulations, seventy-five metres was the maximum limit for a diver operating on air. Sure, there was no hard and fast physiological wall – some divers may function perfectly well beneath that depth; others may not. And the reason why they wouldn't be functioning properly is nitrogen narcosis. At eighty-three metres on air, a diver might be hard pressed to tie a shoelace let alone play plumber on a broken dam. Just reaching the bottom would set a new depth record for diving in the Southern Hemisphere. Ultimately, it was a job that nobody else in the world would do on air.

Three-quarters of the air we breathe is nitrogen, and we use none of it. It goes in and out of our lungs without ever entering our bloodstream. Under water things change: with the increased pressure blood begins to absorb nitrogen. This will affect the brain like nitrous oxide, the happy gas supplied by dentists and hospitals. The deeper the water, the more pronounced the effect. The rough guide is the 'martini rule': every ten metres down, which adds one extra atmosphere of pressure, is like drinking one martini. By that gauge, the Eucumbene divers would be operating with eight cocktails under their belts.

The team was put together in Sydney. Each man took simulated dives to ninety metres inside a pressure chamber. If they 'narked' they were taken off the job. What the job was exactly, none of the divers really knew.

'Not at any stage did anybody sit me down, or the rest of us, and say, "This is where we're at, this is how it's happening",' said Doug Moore, a leading seaman at the time. 'We were blundering along.'

The team set up on a pontoon positioned above the submerged tower. A decompression chamber was lowered to a depth of eighteen metres to deal with the other key danger of nitrogen being absorbed by the blood under pressure: the bends. When the pressure comes off, the nitrogen absorbed by the blood will want to revert to gas. Surface too fast and nitrogen bubbles will form and block up blood vessels. The pain can be excruciating. A controlled ascent, with a diver making regular stops, allows the nitrogen to ease its way gently out of the blood via the lungs. Because of the depth and the use of air, narcosis and the bends were the two main limiting factors of the Eucumbene job. The best option was for the men to do fifteen minutes of work at the bottom and then spend ninety minutes decompressing.

None of the divers had 'narked' on the simulated dives in Sydney, but on the job things were different. The whole operation almost came to a halt because nearly all the divers suffered narcosis. They'd declare that a rope had been fixed to an object that needed hauling up by crane when it hadn't, or they'd get themselves tangled up in their lines. Any diver that narked was barred from working below fifty-five metres. There was still plenty of work for them to do, but to be restricted was still a blow to the ego. Ultimately, only two divers were able to function on the very bottom: Jake Linton and Doug Moore. By virtue of some freak genetic endowment, these two men were able to operate under the effects of narcosis, yet even *their* sanity and judgement was questioned at times.

The air at that depth was so thick it felt like they had to drink it into their lungs. It also had an odd effect on their vocal chord – their voices went high-pitched. It made them sound hysterical. Both Linton and Moore at times laboured to convince the dive supervisor up top that they were sane and to let them continue. It was an extremely fine line: both were indeed narked but somehow they could still keep control. Linton experienced a time-delay effect. His body lagged a few seconds behind what his mind was telling it to do. For Moore, time flew. He would surface thinking he could only have spent two minutes on the bottom when he had spent twenty. The main worry with narcosis was that the diver would flatly disobey orders to surface and end up dead. Not wanting a death on their watch, some supervisors were overly twitchy about potential disaster. They would want to yank a diver or send the stand-by down all too quickly. The job was hard enough without hearing someone wrongly accuse you of being narked. Linton refused to dive without having Batterham, whose judgement he trusted, being up top.

Moore was the first to reach the bottom and what he saw puzzled him. On the surface he reported that he'd seen a tractor tyre up against the stop logs. Moore noticed that the engineers from the SMA began to look very uncomfortable. They went into a huddle and then emerged with a confession. For the first time, the divers learned the true nature of their mission.

As the dam had filled, the problem of the leak had grown more worrying. If it wasn't stemmed, no inspection of the gates would be possible. As the water rose, putting the problem further and further from reach, the engineers had grown desperate. They began to throw sandbags, hay bales and God knows what else down the tower, trying to land the trash behind the stop logs and so plug the leak. In the end, they were well and truly stuffed. The dam was full, the leak was as bad as ever, and now the bottom of the tower was filled with all manner of garbage. In order to inspect the gates, they would have to drain the dam of most of its water to provide a safe working depth for regular divers.

That this information had been withheld from them annoyed the divers, but they pressed on and after four months they had cleared the tower and fixed the leak. Both Linton and Moore were awarded the British Empire Medal, as was Norm Jefres, who saved the life of a narked diver who became so badly snagged that he was unable to ascend by himself. The team returned to Sydney and went about their usual business. In their own nonchalant way, they felt lucky that they hadn't lost a man on what was an unnecessarily high-risk job. But within a year, two young members of the Eucumbene team – Kel Creasy and John Ingram – would be killed performing the most routine of duties.

SEVEN
INTO VIETNAM

THE FIRST CLEARANCE divers to enter the Vietnam War had no idea that that's where they were headed. They'd left Australia in early 1966 bound for Singapore, and as far as they knew they were off to spend five months with divers from the Royal Navy's Far East Fleet. They were teaming up with the Brits to salvage a crashed aeroplane and to survey the wreck of the battleship HMS *Prince of Wales*. They would participate in mine location and recovery exercises, and then they would return home. Vietnam wasn't on the radar. The conflict was professionally irrelevant – it was a soldier's war.

Somewhere along the way, the plan changed. Lieutenant Commander Alistair Cuthbert, an English officer on exchange with the Australian Navy, got orders to split his six-man team in two. He took Petty Officer John Kershler and

Able Seaman Paul Wright and boarded HMAS *Melbourne* in Singapore. Two days later the three men were on HMAS *Sydney*, an old aircraft carrier delivering the 1st Australian Task Force to South Vietnam.

This was the *Sydney*'s third such voyage since May 1965, when she took Australia's first infantry battalion to the war. She was dubbed the 'Vung Tau Ferry' after her destination port, and she was never short of company upon arrival. With the rapid build-up of US forces – troop numbers alone went from 16,000 in 1964 to 389,000 in 1966 – Vung Tau became a bustling harbour. A constant stream of freighters and navy vessels poured in to feed the 'Free World' war effort and those bound for Saigon had to anchor in Vung Tau harbour and wait their turn to head upriver. Viet Cong saboteurs suddenly found themselves presented with a wealth of targets. A surge in mine attacks prompted all ships to post sentries to watch for enemy swimmers. In addition to this, naval ships like the *Sydney* would have their hulls and anchor cables checked for mines.

Sydney never lingered in Vung Tau. She entered the anchorage at night, unlit with her crew on high alert. At dawn, choppers would begin taxying troops to and from the Australian Task Force base at Nui Dat while barges got busy discharging her cargo. The old carrier was a hive of activity and was unloaded and loaded in an impressive forty-eight hours. It was during this hectic time that the hull searches had to be carried out. *Sydney* had her own diving team made up of specialist divers – typically a chief, two able seamen CDs and up to five seamen who were training to become

CDs – and about ten 'ship's divers', who were scuba-qualified sailors. The role of Cuthbert's team was to give these guys a hand with the constant searches. Poor visibility, enemy threats and the close proximity of barges to the ship meant this was no easy task. Their work was only interrupted by the ferocious tidal currents.

During one of *Sydney*'s offloading phases, an American forklift driver lost control of his vehicle and it plunged into the sea. A crane operator immediately dropped a heavy cable into the water at the forklift's entry point, and one of *Sydney*'s clearance divers, Chief Petty Officer Len Luhrmann, jumped into the water and followed the line down. A few metres down he was forced to let go – the current was ripping the mask and demand valve from his face. The forklift was gone: in that kind of current, it could have been anywhere between the *Sydney* and the Philippines. For this reason, hulls had to be inspected during the slack-water periods. The divers would do this by way of a 'half-necklace' search. Connected to each other by a buddy line, they went from one end of the ship to the other, swimming in a vertical formation that extended from the waterline to the keel. They swept their hands over the hull's surface as they went to ensure no limpet mines had been attached. One diver was positioned on the other side of the hull to look out for enemy swimmers. This kind of search was done every half hour before the current started to run again.

When the last barge was loaded, Cuthbert ordered his men to board it. Unable to return to Singapore the way they had come, they intended to fly back. So at one in the morning they went ashore and slept on the beach. When dawn came they hitched a ride on a US chopper into Saigon.

Getting out of Vietnam proved more difficult than expected: the men had entered without passports and, of course, had no visas. This was a problem that only a grid-lock of bureaucracy could fix. Cuthbert made good use of the hold-up; he sought to find out what the US Navy was dealing with in terms of explosive ordnance disposal (EOD), the new name given to 'bomb and mine disposal'. When he visited their EOD headquarters in Saigon, the Americans told him they were undermanned. They had six men up in Da Nang, just below the demilitarised zone (DMZ), and four in Sai-gon. Every month across the whole of South Vietnam there were around 380 'incidents' reported – Viet Cong mines, booby-traps, suspect ordnance. Naturally, they couldn't han-dle them all. Cuthbert's host, Captain J. T. Shepard, asked if Australia was thinking of sending a navy EOD team to Vietnam full-time. The Australian government, and the Royal Australian Navy for that matter, had no such intention whatsoever. Cuthbert would grow resolved to change their minds. Meantime, he saw an opportunity for his men to gain some invaluable experience. He proposed a short-term visit by his team to help the Americans out. The offer was grate-fully accepted. Three weeks later he was back with his full contingent.

They spent just over a week with the Americans but Cuth-bert's enterprise was vindicated. He and his men witnessed the new age of war first-hand. Up until that moment, the Australian and British outlook regarding EOD was turned backwards. They were still focussed on World War II ordnance – Japanese, American and German mines mostly. In Vietnam, the Americans were engaged in a guerrilla war and being exposed to new threats – a horridly novel mix of homemade bombs, booby-traps and Chinese Communist (ChiCom) weaponry. Flying his men from Singapore to Saigon, Cuthbert took Australian clearance diving forward twenty years. Perhaps this was his motivation all along.

The men had no idea what to expect. They travelled from Saigon to Nha Be, a riverside US naval base ten kilometres south of the capital. They had no weapons and no gear, not even a pair of fins. While on exercise in Singapore, they were very much an extension of the Royal Navy. There was little difference in the way they operated, the way they'd been trained and the gear that they used. And diving was the core of everything they did. Now, suddenly, they were in a war alongside the Yanks. They were land-based with not a ripple of ocean to be seen. They were in the thick of a jungle laced by muddy water, having to get by on whatever gear and hospitality their American friends could provide.

The Nha Be base at the time was just a huddle of tents from which the US Navy began to launch patrols into the network of waterways and to provide escorts for boats travelling from Vung Tau to Saigon. Between Nha Be and Vung Tau on the coast was 400 square kilometres of notorious swampland called Rung Sat, the 'Forest of Assassins'. The name was old, coined when the wet, muddy, impenetrable wilderness of the Mekong Delta served as a haven for criminals, smugglers and pirates. Under the French, the channel network was enhanced to help drainage and boost rice production. As the Vietnam War intensified, the Viet Cong moved freely through the area, smuggling weapons, garnering support in villages and launching strikes on the increasing number of foreign craft. Using small arms, rockets, rocket-propelled grenades, mortars and mines, they attacked Saigon-bound supply ships before melting into the maze of canals. The US River Patrol Squadron and a Navy SEAL team were moved into Nha Be to hunt them down.

The first job for Cuthbert's team was to board a grounded freighter that had hit a mine. The Viet Cong had booby-trapped the ship to hinder American attempts to salvage the cargo. The divers were called upon to clear the devices.

Floating mines were quite common, and whenever they were found intact the Australians were sent to dispose of them. They had no tools to dismantle the homemade bombs but that didn't matter – they would just find an empty stretch of riverbank, fix charges to the device and blow it up. Every day the divers conducted hull and cable searches on the ships moored at Nha Be. And on occasion they ventured out with the SEALs.

Upon meeting the elite unit, Kershler noticed that some wore unusual pieces of jewellery on their dog tags. He could see that they were pieces of shrivelled meat but had no idea what they were, so he asked. He was told that they were the ears of Viet Cong the men had killed. The Australian felt extremely naïve. He'd left home thinking he'd be deep diving in crystal-clear tropical waters and enjoying a few sundowners with his Pommy counterparts, and here he was in a hatefully intimate guerrilla war. With the divers taking up the EOD tasks, the SEALs were freed up to go hunt. They were like no men Kershler had ever met. If he didn't know better, he would have sworn they'd been given a choice back home: Vietnam or prison.

Once the week was up the team returned to Singapore. There was no question in Cuthbert's mind that the excursion was a success. His men had gained operational experience in a hostile environment, and the Americans were left wanting more. In his Report of Proceedings, Cuthbert pushed the case for a six-man clearance diving team to be deployed to Vietnam. They could help look after the *Sydney* whenever she was in Vung Tau and take some load off the swamped US EOD guys. Best of all, it was a bargain commitment for a cautious government – a small, solid contribution for not much money.

Cuthbert was soon brought down to earth. It seemed that while his navy superiors were aware of his Saigon forays, the Holt government was not, and the news that there had been a RAN diving team operating on the ground in Vietnam did not go down well at all. The war was still popular at the time, but not *that* popular. For all the public support for fighting the commies (a stridently anti-war Labor was trounced in the 1966 federal election), the Holt government was reluctant to commit more Australian lives to the cause. It feared, rightly, that Vietnam was a quicksand conflict – and here was navy sending men in willy nilly. Cuthbert received an obligatory rap over the knuckles, but he did Holt a favour. At the time, Canberra was being urged by Washington to do more in

Vietnam, and Cuthbert's proposal began to gain favour and then approval. In February 1967, eight months after Cuthbert's team left Nha Be, the first contingent of RAN clearance divers specially trained for the Vietnam conflict flew into Saigon. The divers would stay for four years, through eight successive contingents, and what they accomplished and learned would have lasting consequences. During Vietnam, the unique character of the Australian clearance diving branch emerged: contemporary and versatile, there was simply no other military outfit in the world like it. After Vietnam, there was no more looking back. The branch had forged its own identity. And that must have made Cuthbert proud.

≈

Mick Shotter was a twenty-nine-year-old lieutenant going about his business at *Rushcutter* when Lieutenant Commander Titcombe called him over.

'You're going to Vietnam,' Titcombe said quietly. 'Keep it under your hat. It's still highly classified.' Shotter had no idea what Titcombe was on about. He knew there was a war on, but navy had done well to keep the decision to deploy a clearance diving team secret. Shotter had just returned from a year serving in Malaysia. Before that he was in Perth. 'Vietnam' was just the label on his next job. That was the way it was for the 'bubblies', as divers called themselves. They were a real-life McHales' Navy: a maverick but crafty lot that would find themselves on all manner of weird and wonderful jobs. They never knew what they'd be doing next. Cuthbert's expedition, which had become an open secret, was a case in point. The bubblies admired what he did yet considered it to be no great surprise: getting a bit 'out there' was kind of the diver's norm. And if the navy wanted Shotter to go to Vietnam in command of a diving team, then that's what he'd be doing.

Shotter's team had already been hand picked. Senior men who knew the young officer well were consulted about candidates for the five other positions – they wanted them to be men Shotter himself would want. This small unit was going to spend six months at war together. Integrity of the command chain was all, and cultural fit mattered a great deal. The navy had only just brought into being two Sydney-based clearance diving teams – CDT1 and CDT2 – which all qualified divers became members of unless they got a ship's posting, went on exchange to the UK or worked at the dive school. Shotter's five men were picked from all quarters. They were called CDT3, or Team 3, the branch's go-to-war team, and they were the first of forty-nine men to be selected.

Preparation for the eight contingents sent varied a little over time, but all of them were put through a four- to six-month work-up before deployment. First there was Vietnam-specific EOD training. Then at the army's Jungle Training Centre in Canungra, Queensland, they were taught how to shoot, patrol and fight a field battle. Then came intelligence briefings. On top of that the 'upper management' – the lieutenant and petty officer – were put through a 'code-of-conduct' course, an excoriating lesson on what to expect if you were caught by Asian commies. Borrowed from the US Army, the course was a pre-emptive move to uphold the operational integrity of the Australian forces. During the Korean War, one in three American prisoners were persuaded by way of brutality or favour to collaborate with their Korean and Chinese captors. They were simply not equipped to deal with psychological manipulation. Effectively rewired, they turned against country, against fellow prisoners and became supplicant propaganda tools. Vietnam was another Cold War proxy. There was every reason to expect POWs to be exploited for both tactical and ideological advantage. Coping with torture, giving nothing away under extreme duress and accepting no favours in hellish conditions were skills that could be, to some degree, learned.

Originally, the men were 'held prisoner' in the century-old tunnels of the Middle Head fortifications that once guarded Sydney Harbour. On release the 'captives' were instructed to warn their men about commie prison camps without ever revealing how they came across such knowledge. The 'code-of-conduct' course 'did not exist'. As the war progressed, the training evolved and the course became more elaborate. By the time the seventh contingent was on its work-up, men were given a train ticket to Adelaide and told there was another course they had to do. Reaching Woodside Barracks, they were ushered into a room with Vietnam-bound army officers. They were all told to be seated for a film presentation. When the lights were turned off, the word 'Captured!' appeared on the screen. Suddenly, Asian-looking men dressed in black stormed into the room shouting and waving guns. They rounded up the confused men, put hoods over their heads, marched them outside and shoved them into trucks. The vehicles left the base, drove around for a good while and then returned. When their hoods were finally removed, the men found themselves in a replica Viet Cong prison camp. They were issued with clothes that didn't fit and pairs of boots that weren't even a left and a right, let alone the same size. They were locked into cells and fed meagre rations of rice. The guards kept them awake at night by dragging batons against the corrugated iron walls and playing Chinese opera music over the camp's loudspeakers. They were interrogated repeatedly – the contents of their confiscated wallets used against them – and humiliated on the parade ground. They were made to learn Mao's *Little Red Book*, a collection of quotations from the Chairman, by heart. Individuals were taken out and 'shot' for trite breaches of conduct, a drama seen in silhouette on the tent wall. Some were thrown into a well. A lid was fitted over the top before water started rushing in from below. The divers knew the air pressure would prevent the water from rising perilously high. Soldiers didn't. By this stage few men retained a full grip on reality. Those who broke down were carted away, and those who hung on found it harder and harder to keep believing that this was all an exercise conducted by their countrymen in Australia. Many started to plan their escape. Finally, when the whole bizarre production came to an end, every inductee took one message deeply to heart: never, ever get caught – pass it on.

Shotter's team landed in Saigon on 6 February 1967. They spent a week there being briefed and taken out on jobs. Although they would work closely with the Americans, Team

3 was an independent entity. The Yanks had asked them to take care of ship security and EOD matters in the Vung Tau area as part of Operation Stable Door, so they made their way down to the coast with a US Navy chief petty officer, trying to find somewhere among the American bases to set up camp. They ended up on top of Nui Lon Mountain, aka VC Hill, with a sweeping view over Vung Tau harbour. This was where US Navy had set up the Harbor Entrance Control Post, which maintained constant radar and visual surveillance of the harbour. The command centre staff had recently relocated, and they suggested the Australians could take their former quarters next door – a bunker that was part of an old French fort. It was little more than a concrete box, but it would do.

From the first night the Australian divers were in the thick of it. Some Americans asked the newcomers to go and take a look at an unmanned boat that was drifting suspiciously through the anchorage. The Viet Cong were known to fill boats with explosives and set them adrift. They would initiate the charge remotely when the vessel came to rest against a target. Shotter's team took a boat out and boarded the drifter. They found nothing suspicious on board and towed it clear of the anchorage.

Right from the start the Americans treated Team 3 like one of their own, outfitting them with sunglasses, watches, greens and cammies to add to the kit they'd already been supplied by the Australian navy. The US Navy ensured that they had everything they needed to do their job. Their jeep, truck, scuba gear, compressor, EOD tools, rubber duckie and

Boston Whaler boats, underwater sonar – all were provided by the Americans. 'If *their* blokes had it, it was a fair bet that *we'd* get it,' said Shotter.

Food was supplied by the Australian army, which was based in Nui Dat, thirty kilometres north-east of Vung Tau. Included in their stores was a ration of beer – two cans per man per day. When setting up their rations account with the army, Shotter was asked how many men his unit contained. He replied that he couldn't really say; it was still classified information, which was stretching the truth. The soldier suggested that if he started guessing, Shotter could tell him when he was in the ballpark. He started counting. When he got to fifteen, Shotter said, 'That's close enough.' In no time, Team 3 had more beer than they knew what to do with, which of course was the plan. The divers were determined to turn their concrete bunker into a home, replete with bar, and for that they needed a self-improvement fund. Shotter and his petty officer, Dick Clark, had figured that beer was the answer.

Victoria Bitter went down very well with the Americans, and there seemed no end to what a slab or two could buy. One day the divers wheeled in a vending machine and filled it with 220 cans. More cartons were traded for fans, food and whatever else the Australians needed. As one contingent followed the next and continued the enhancements, the divers' bunker, now known as The Cave, grew into a minor legend. Beer brought them timber from contractors down the road, which they used to panel the walls and build a bench bar. They got floor tiles off the *Sydney*. An air conditioner was installed courtesy of US military police down in the harbour who happened to know where there was a barge full of them. The walls became plastered with centrefolds, and all over the joint were pieces of ordnance. Some were trophies, others were used for disposal demonstrations. The first guests through the door were the neighbours, and over the years a host of characters propped themselves up against the bar, from CIA agents to chopper pilots to war-hooked special ops commanders. The divers once threw a New Zealand SAS outfit a farewell hangi. It almost killed the lot of them, so bad was the food poisoning. The bar was basically open all the time, but it wasn't about getting pissed every night. Being on constant duty meant that most of the time they had to stay dry.

Shotter's team filled two roles within the US Navy's harbour protection operation. As EOD specialists, they were the go-to guys for any ordnance issues – unexploded shells, enemy bombs, booby-traps, caches of ammo and car bombs. But their primary role was the safety of the Vung Tau anchorage. Beyond these main duties, there were regular diving tasks to recover weapons, equipment and corpses.

Lack of dock space meant that cargo destined for the several bases in the Vung Tau area had to be shuttled to the beach by barges. Meanwhile, ships bound for Saigon had to wait their turn to take one of the two channels that wound their way through the Rung Sat. At any given time there were dozens of naval ships and freighters anchored in the harbour. It was up to the divers to inspect their hulls and anchor chains for mines.

They didn't know it at the time but Team 3 had a direct enemy: the swimmer sappers of Group 10, a 600-strong unit of Viet Cong that operated in and around the Rung Sat. The Viet Cong always claimed to be an insurgency, and with fair cause given the odious regime governing South Vietnam, but in fact it was always a proxy of the North Vietnamese communists, who in turn were backed by the USSR and China. In January 1966, as the US commitment in the south was ramping up, the North Vietnamese created the 126 Naval Sapper Regiment. This was a selective special operations unit focussed on infiltration and sabotage. Members underwent six months' training, and some instructors attended courses in China and the Soviet Union. Their expertise, and at times personnel, was sent south to equip Group 10 with swimmer sappers. It was their handiwork that pressed the need for round-the-clock ship defence in Vung Tau and other ports in South Vietnam.

During 1966, Group 10 carried out twenty-seven mining attacks in the Vung Tau area alone. In August, they claimed their first American victim, the 8500-ton *Baton Rouge Victory*, after placing a limpet mine on its hull. The blast killed seven men. The water was too shallow for the vessel to sink completely, but it managed to move aside to leave the channel clear. The material cost of the strike was a month's rations for the entire US 4th Division, plus water damage to personnel carriers, aircraft and other stores. If left unopposed, Group 10 could choke the Rung Sat channels with half-submerged hulks and cut off surface supply to Saigon altogether.

Many of Group 10's mines were homemade. A common

device comprised of two floating mines linked by a long rope that was released upriver from a ship. The mines would drift past on either side of the anchor chain; when the rope snagged, the explosives would sweep in on either side of the ship's hull and detonate on impact.

The enemy's window of opportunity was during the tide's slackwater period, when they could plant a limpet mine on a ship without fear of being swept away. This window coincided with the clearance team's searches, when three members would head out to the anchorage in a runabout. Initially they wore scuba gear, but before long they ditched the cylinders and fins. Overalls and a mask were all they needed, and an anchor cable search was done on a breath-hold. This mirrored how the enemy dived – nothing but a mask, snorkel and a lungful of air. Once they got into their stride they conducted 200 searches a month; in May, Shotter's men set a Team 3 record in Vietnam of 327 searches. At first the inspections were conducted during the day, but then the teams went out at night to be present when the enemy was most active. On the vast majority nothing was found but there was nothing blasé about a search. It was a nerve-racking experience from the moment they left base.

Searching at night meant that the divers had to break curfew to get down to the harbour. Two of them would jump into the jeep, and once they were out the gate they felt like they were a target. The odd warning of an impending VC attack served to remind them that the enemy was free to walk up and knock on their bunker's door. There were only two routes to the beach, so options for deception were limited.

One diver would drive while the other rode shotgun with a cocked submachine gun. An umbrella curfew was in place, on the streets and on the water. Sentries were on edge and no one was obliged to get all your particulars before shooting in this 'free fire' zone. Passing through the town, Vung Tau's vibrant nightlife of a few hours earlier (it was where both Allied troops and Viet Cong went for R and R) was gone. No open bars, no strains of Vietnamese cover bands, no bar girls beckoning you to buy them a Saigon tea, the high-priced drink that was a docket for their company. The streets were dark and dead still.

From the beach the team would head out to the anchorage with lights flashing. The mood on the harbour was always tense but more so after mining attacks. There could be up to forty ships anchored there at one time, and the team had to approach each vessel cautiously. During the fourth contingent's tenure, an American EOD swimmer was shot and killed by a USN sentry in Cam Ranh Bay, north of Vung Tau. Usually, the navy ships were safer because the old rust-bucket merchant ships were often crewed by men who had never found themselves sitting ducks in a war zone before and who spoke no English. They'd open fire on a coconut, a box – anything on the water that might provide cover for a swimmer. The divers used a loudhailer to explain who they were and that they intended to search the rudder and anchor cable, and they made damn sure their message was fully understood. This sometimes meant going around a ship and addressing, or even waking up, the sentries on the stern, the bridge and the bow. Shouting and warning shots were the norm. Only after they received satisfactory acknowledgements would the men begin diving. When the current started to run they'd have to jump into the water ahead of the anchor chain, grab it as they were swept past and then swim down into the murky depths as far as they could.

The Americans had been generous from the outset and Shotter's team was always willing to return the favour. As the Yanks discovered more about the divers' skills range, they called on them to help out on plenty of odd jobs, mostly EOD work. Without fail they would be assigned a protection force to go with them for cover while they were in the water. Shotter's men never refused a job, and so it wasn't long before they were operating in breach of conditions set down by the casualty-conscious Australian Navy. Back in Australia the navy brass had made themselves pretty clear to Shotter: don't work with the SEALs, stay out of Cambodia and keep your men safe. By the time Team 3 had been in Vietnam a week, Shotter's men had been out with the SEALs, sniffing around enemy territory. As for Cambodia, well, they got close enough. The team were EOD specialists in a war zone, and their Allies needed their help. They were not about to turn them down.

'They [the navy] relied on us to use our brains, and we did,' said Shotter. 'I was of the assumption that we were sent to do a job – and that's what we were going to do.'

And sometimes only those on the ground can tell what that job is. Once Shotter and two of his men were taken a few kilometres north-east of Saigon to check a bridge that had been destroyed by the Viet Cong. Before any rebuilding could begin, the remains of the bridge had to be checked for booby-traps. The party saw quite a few locals in the rice paddies when they arrived. By the time they were ready to dive, the fields were empty. A Vietnamese man crossed from the far side, saying he had a message from the Viet Cong: they dared the foreigners to come to their village and fight. There were three divers, a US Special Forces major, a USN chief petty officer and about five others. The men decided to accept the challenge. When they reached the village, all they found were a few booby-traps. The place had been recently evacuated. Shotter knew they were being watched.

'They let us in and let us out,' said Shotter. 'Didn't shoot at anybody. I guess they were trying to figure out if we were stupid or brave enough to go. I had faith in our guys, and I assumed this major knew what he was talking about, so we went.'

There were two other US military operations Team 3 was involved in: Market Time and Game Warden. The former was an effort to intercept vessels supplying weapons and ammunition to the Viet Cong. Up until 1966, the North Vietnamese sent most of their arms contributions down the coast by boat. There were so many fishing vessels and sampans that this was a fairly simple task. But with Market Time, boats were stopped and searched, and curfews were enforced, and so Hanoi was compelled to rely more heavily on the Ho Chi Minh Trail to resupply the Viet Cong. Operation Game Warden was an effort to deny the Viet Cong the use of the Rung Sat and Mekong Delta. The divers didn't really care what the overall operation was called; when the US asked them to handle any EOD issues they obliged. As a result, Team 3 took part in sweeps, patrols and beach landings run by the Americans with the South Vietnamese navy – the 'Junk Force'.

In May, a US Army Huey helicopter crashed upside down into a river north-east of Saigon. Team 3 was requested to dive on the sunken chopper, retrieve the bodies of the two missing crew, salvage all weapons and secure the recovery straps so that the Huey could be lifted free. Travelling light, Shotter and his two leading seamen, Phil Kember and Peter Boettcher, packed just one dive kit between them along with their combat gear and boarded a chopper.

The crash site was in the middle of an ongoing battle. The pilot flew in under the arc of artillery shells. When they touched down, the shells were landing on enemy positions just a hundred metres away. As the divers got themselves ready, two battalions of US infantry had their backs. Kember was tasked with the dive. In near zero visibility he found and retrieved one body but couldn't locate the other. He then salvaged the weapons and while doing so found the other body. The corpse had stiffened and become wedged in the cabin. Unable to shift it, Kember proceeded to secure the recovery straps. That's when he got stuck, his cylinders snagging on loose wires. He couldn't reach up to free himself, and his initial attempts to manoeuvre free failed. The fact that he had the only dive kit hit home. Even though his comrades were just metres away he was on his own. Keeping calm, he allowed himself to sink down. Fortunately, he felt no pull from wires. He backed out and surfaced, telling Shotter that for a minute there he thought there would be an extra body to recover. He then descended again and ran the straps through the cabin, this time rolling over to keep his cylinders clear of the wires, and a Chinook lifted the Huey out of the water. For this deed Kember was awarded the Distinguished Service Medal.

A month later, the monsoon season settled in. The wild conditions made ship searches, as well as ship attacks, nigh impossible. Team 3 was put on hold unless an emergency broke out. In the rough conditions boats and buoys broke their moorings and, with rumours of an impending Viet Cong attack rife, Shotter's men were called out at all hours to inspect one item or another. All proved to be 'false alarms', a term that hints at an overreaction and dilutes the intense and courageous process required to reach each and every safe verdict. 'False alarm' was pure hindsight, comfort after the event. Before that it was a cold-sweat ordeal spent dreading an explosion; it was an enemy bomb waiting to blow up in your face.

EIGHT
BIN THE RULEBOOK

FROM THE MOMENT word spread about Shotter's team going to Vietnam, the ninety-odd divers who'd missed out wanted in. They'd have been busting to go if the war was in Siberia. They didn't care about the South Vietnamese people or in what ways, if any, their hopes or ideology differed from their northern brethren. The average diver may well have believed in the domino theory of communism's spread, a concept that was hardly a stretch of the imagination. Japan had shown how quickly the chain of South-East Asian colonies could fall; Australia had fought communist forces in Korea and Malaya; and the Indonesian communist party had the ear of the Sukarno regime, as did the Soviets and Chinese. Direct military conflict with Sukarno's forces in Borneo and 'aggressive communism' in Indochina prompted

Prime Minister Menzies to reintroduce conscription in 1964. Barely a conflict existed that didn't have a Cold War angle. And if democracy needed defending against communism in Vietnam, then any serviceman might feel duty and honour bound to go. More than anything, though, the divers' enthusiasm sprang from pure ambition – personal and professional. War was a chance to show what they were made of.

The youngest among them had been drawn into the branch by the clearance diving presentation at recruit school. They'd been shown a film on the daring exploits of the Italian charioteers. They were told about ship attacks, beach reconnaissance, rendering mines safe and general-purpose diving. Navy divers had won world acclaim at Lake Eucumbene, and their daring deeds had made more headlines since. During 1960–61 alone, they'd been called upon to conduct salvage operations on no less than four aircraft crashes: an Ansett-ANA helicopter, a TAA Fokker Friendship, an RAAF Sabre jet and an Ansett Vickers Viscount. This was why the young men had joined – clearance diving was adventurous, mysterious and dangerous. The older divers were veterans of those arduous and grim civilian jobs that had lit the imaginations of their juniors.

What every diver, young and old, had in common was that they had gone through hell to join. Once in, they had continued to train like mad to keep their skills sharp. But training was training – war was the ultimate proficiency test. Even in New Guinea, where they were dismantling and disposing of Japanese and American bombs, they could consult a manual and they never had to fear a sniper's bullet.

On a broader level there was a tribal cause. Cuthbert's adventures did not constitute a deployment. The branch – the Royal Australian Navy clearance divers – had not officially been blooded in war. Vietnam was to be its baptism of fire. For men who held the unit close to heart, playing a role in this monumental event seemed almost a right. But you could only wait to be chosen. For those who were, no amount of training prepared them for the experience.

'It was one big drunken party on the way up,' remembered Jeff Garrett, an able seaman with the fifth Team 3 contingent. 'Free booze from Qantas and we drank all night.'

The Qantas charter stopped in Singapore at around two in the morning. Being in what was supposed to be 'neutral territory', the soldiers and six divers had to don a casual shirt before they disembarked. But what else could a planeload of young men wearing Hawaiian shirts and jungle boots be but troops bound for Vietnam? While the soldiers waited at the airport, Garrett and the two other junior members of his team scaled the airport's three-metre high brick wall and made a run for it. They were sailors – many ports in Asia were already familiar to them. They made a beeline for Singapore's red-light district and returned just in time to board.

Once back in the air, the mood in the plane turned sombre. When the captain announced they were approaching Vietnam, Garrett's imagination went into overdrive. He looked out the window, thinking he might spot destroyers firing into the coastline. He saw none. Over land, he scanned the darkness for flashes, explosions, smoke – any signs of war. Nothing. Reality only struck when they set foot upon the tarmac in Saigon.

The new arrivals gagged in the steam-bath heat, but it was the sight and sound of the phenomenal US war machine that really took their breath away. There was hardly a busier airport in the world and surely no louder place on earth. All around them swirled jets, bombers, air freighters, transport planes, Chinooks, trucks, jeeps, artillery and men. Such a stupendous display of muscle and firepower was intimidating to behold, even for allies.

The divers were taken by bus through Saigon to the US Navy EOD headquarters. They stared out at the strange city through wire mesh. It was unsettling to think that the windows had been removed and grills fitted to stop people from lobbing grenades into their laps. Preconceived ideas about 'guerrilla warfare' and 'the absence of a front line' acquired real and dramatic meaning.

To Pat Zegenhagen, an able seaman with the second contingent, the show-and-tell put on for them was terrifying. Even for the last contingents, very few Vietnam-specific EOD samples had made it back to Australia. Their education mostly drew off photographs and first-hand descriptions. The most practical lesson they learned was one they'd taught each other: always be on alert. Around the workshop in *Rushcutter*, they had to be constantly wary of booby-traps. Open a coffee jar, biscuit tin, locker or even a *Playboy* magazine without checking it over first and a small charge was

Lieutenant Commander John Stuart Mould prepares to dive. (Leon Goldsworthy/ AWM P03434.019)

(Above) Lieutenant Commander Leon Verdi Goldsworthy holds a fuse he has just removed from a parachute mine. (AWM P03434.002)

(Left) Lieutenant Hugh Randall Syme beside a magnetic parachute mine. (Leon Goldsworthy/ AWM P03434.001)

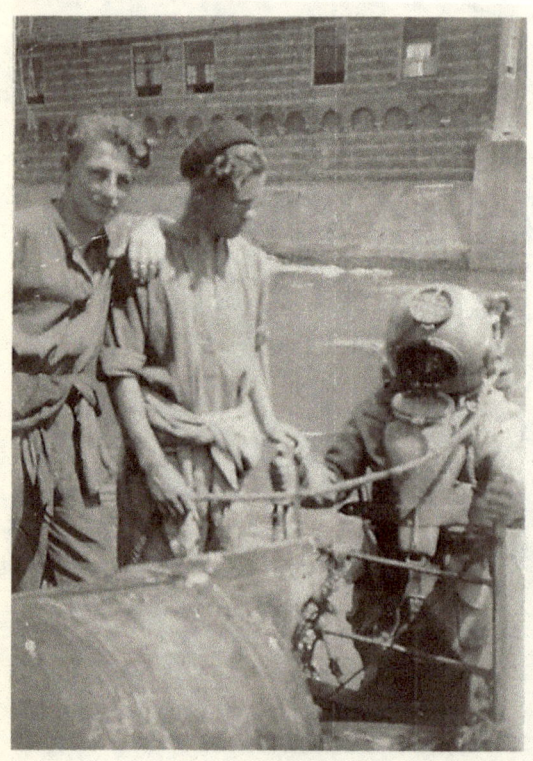

A magnetic mine recovered intact was a 'free gift from Germany' that allowed British scientists to study its workings. (AWM P05468.012)

British P Party diver Mike Connolly emerges from the water in Amsterdam wearing the Mould Mine Recovery Suit. (Mike Connolly)

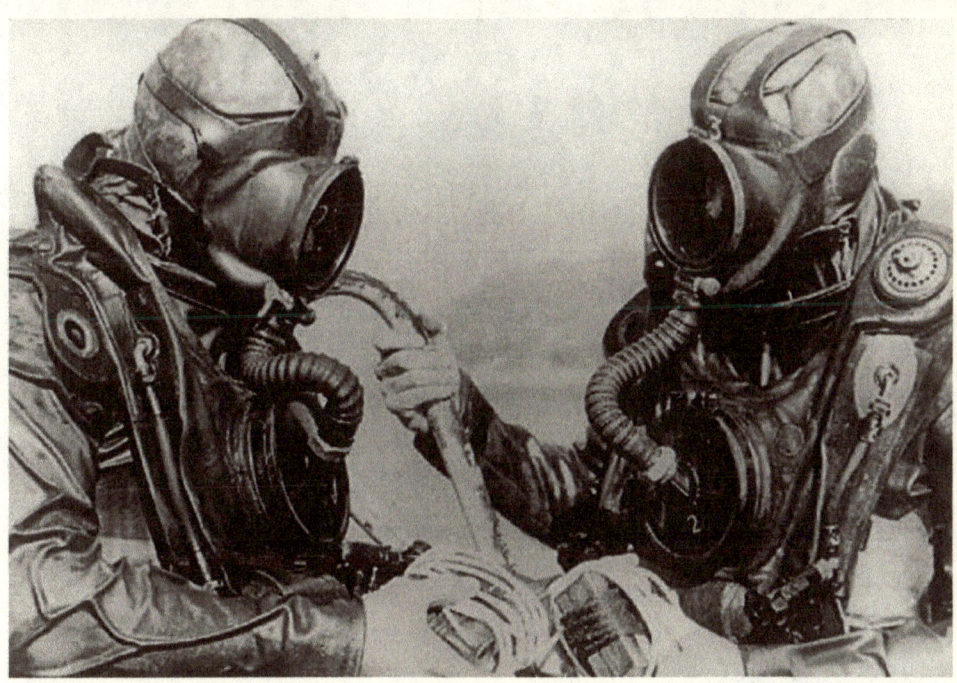

The Royal Australian Navy's new specialist divers take to the water in Port Phillip Bay, 1956. (AWM 304811)

Looking like creatures from the Black Lagoon, 'navy frogmen' captured public imagination after the Second World War. These divers hold explosives for demolitions training, and maybe to catch a few fish. (RAN Clearance Divers Association website)

Diving School instructors, 1958. Standing, left to right: Alex Donald, Bill Fitzgerald, Alan Jones, Colonel Carr. Seated, left to right: Dixie Foord, Darky Voght, Lieutenant Commander Morty Drummond RN. (RAN Clearance Divers Association website)

(Above) Lieutenant Commander Batterham helps a diver as he prepares to dive to record depths on air at Lake Eucumbene. The stand-by diver to the right will remain kitted up on the surface, ready to dive in case of a mishap. (Doug Moore)

(Left) The sixty-seven-metre-high straining tower at Lake Eucumbene. By the time the divers arrived, the top of the tower was sixteen metres under water. (Doug Moore)

There's a trail here somewhere. South Vietnamese troops under US command with Australian divers as EOD specialists head into enemy territory. (Barry Bailey)

North Vietnamese artillery attacks on the Dong Ha ammo dump left an extremely hazardous clean-up job. (John Kershler)

The bunker that became a legend: The Cave. (RAN Clearance Divers Association website)

A booby-trapped 82mm mortar. The VC covered the pit so that, when stepped on, the wires pull on the detonator. This trap was discovered after a US soldier trod right on the edge of the pit. He escaped with legs and life intact. (John Kershler)

Placing a charge in a VC bunker. (Barry Bailey)

The Patrol Craft, Fast (PCF), or Swift boats, were the backbone of the US 'Brown-Water Navy', forever running the gauntlet along the thin channels that lace the Mekong Delta. (John Kershler)

Swift boats cover Australian divers as they check a VC-built log barricade for mines before destroying it. (Fred Adler/AWM P03654.090)

American, Australian and South Vietnamese divers weave hose charges through a log barricade built by the VC to ambush patrols. (Fred Adler/ AWM P03654.099)

VC barricade blown sky high. (Fred Adler/ AWM P03654.087)

A gunner lets rip with suppression fire to cover Team 3 divers. (RAN/AWM NAVYM0459/07)

Infiltration training as part of a Maritime Tactical Operations exercise. (RAN)

Fast-roping training at the 2011 RIMPAC multi-national naval exercise in Hawaii. (RAN)

A member of Perth's Team 4 takes part in Maritime Tactical Operations training. (RAN)

With his gear securely cached under water, a diver hooks a caving ladder onto the structure to allow for a surprise attack. (RAN)

No bubbles break the surface when using oxygen rebreathers. During covert dive training, the floats help maintain a safe depth while the lead diver can focus on the compass bearing. (RAN)

Surface-fed deep-diving for the modern era. (RAN)

Mine countermeasures operations in Umm Qasr. On their very first dive, working by feel in the murky water, the Australians found Iraqi mines. (Scott Craig)

(Above) Members of Team 3 decide how they will dispose of this cache of Iraqi mines. (Scott Craig)

(Left) Clearance diver on security detail in Umm Qasr, Iraq. (Scott Craig)

Maritime Tactical Operations training: making a 'back of beach' incursion into an enemy beach ahead of an amphibious landing. (RAN Clearance Divers Association website)

Upwardly mobile in Sydney Harbour. (RAN Clearance Divers Association website)

Members of TAG East blast their way into the 'method of entry house' at Holsworthy.
(RAN Clearance Divers Association website)

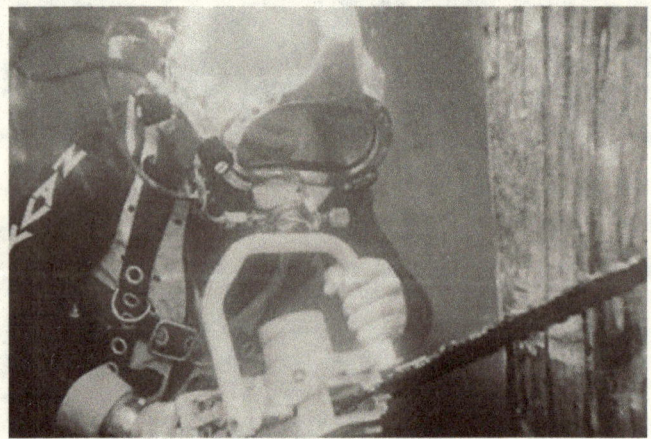

For many, this is the best gig in the branch – Underwater Battle Damage Repair.
(RAN Clearance Divers Association website)

A diver uses sonar to locate objects of interest. (RAN Clearance Divers Association website)

Petty Officer Lane Patterson wins the day after disposing of a very large pipe bomb laid by the Taliban in Afghanistan. (Lane Patterson)

Leading Seaman Jeremy Thomas helps Patterson into the bomb suit as he prepares to head down range to follow up on the work the robot (in background) has done on an IED. (Lane Patterson)

Diver hopefuls undertake yet another evolution during CDAT, where they have to swim under one Zodiac, clamber over another, swim back to the wharf, and do it again and again. (Gregor Salmon)

Take it while you can. CDAT recruits snatch a few minutes' shut-eye as the launch ferries them to their next task. (Gregor Salmon)

likely to go off. The explosion was shockingly loud and hot enough to singe eyebrows.

'It all helped prepare us for the real thing, the world of "complete success or absolute failure",' said Zegenhagen in a written interview. The last phrase was an EOD mantra, like 'one flash and you're ash'. But for all Zegenhagen's training, the EOD indoctrination in Saigon was a chilling reality check.

'I arrived in Vietnam reasonably confident that I could handle any situation. That blissful ignorance was dispelled somewhat in the briefing room our first day.'

On display were the kinds of ChiCom ordnance and traps he needed to become familiar with and learn how to strip, pronto. They ranged from modern to downright medieval. There were the homemade floating mines with protruding tin cans that detonated the main charge when they struck a ship's hull. There was a sickening array of booby-traps. Many were constructed using punji stakes, bamboo skewers sharpened to a needle point. The Viet Cong would stick them upright in the bottom of a concealed hole or else angled downward so that the enemy would have to free anyone caught. The tips of the punji stakes were often dipped in human faeces to promote infection. There were trip-wire traps that fired mortars from point-blank range into the victim's legs.

A stopover in Nui Dat brought the divers into contact with the Australian combat troops, a sobering sight for the new bloods. 'They looked tired,' said Garrett. 'The guys were in army greens but there was nothing pressed, cleaned and starched. Their hats were worn and bleached. We knew then we were really in a war.'

Another Caribou helicopter ride and they were in Vung Tau, where a couple of members of the old team were there to greet them. Typically, these guys were laid back and in high spirits. They were heading home in a matter of days. En route to the base they would stop here and there to say their goodbyes to friends. Once they had all reached The Cave, it was into casual clothes for a welcome beer and barbecue. Later they would grab a few tinnies and walk further up the hill to watch the war. As they looked south-west across the Mekong Delta, they could see American forces attacking enemy positions. Rockets arced inland. Flares lit up the Forest of Assassins like it was a fairground. And if the 'Snoopies' were out – the AC-47 planes that circled their targets and stitched 18,000 rounds a minute into them – they put on a spectacular show, cutting a cone of red-hot tracer fire into the night. It was gripping, surreal entertainment.

If the Saigon briefing was a reality check, the two-week handover period was a radical re-education. In the training environment, bomb and mine disposal was a strict, orderly discipline. Students followed carefully in precedent's footsteps, and they learned to do so literally blindfolded. In Vietnam, they were told that the only place for the EOD rulebook was the bin. The new boys thought they'd walked into a madhouse.

'When our contingent first arrived at The Cave, someone was in the accommodation area drilling a hole into a bomb fuse with an electric drill,' wrote Zegenhagen. Stripping live ordnance in a confined space was an outrageous violation of protocol. 'An accident could have wiped out the entire team.'

At any given time there might be two divers at the bench pulling apart rocket propelled grenades as though they were no more harmful than transistor radios.

'We were shocked by the things the bloody mad bastards of the previous team were doing,' said Aldenhoven, 'and yet we became just like them.'

In truth, it was a case of adapting more than forgetting. During those two weeks the outgoing men took the relief team under their wing, showing them the ropes, and the range of ChiCom, Soviet and Allied ordnance kept on display inside The Cave. More live ordnance was stored in another bunker nearby. There were orthodox stripping methods that would please an EOD assessor back home, and then there were more feral methods, products of field-sharpened cunning. No EOD manual, for instance, was going to show you how to strip an anti-personnel mine with a can-opener.

The men arrived knowing that they were the EOD response team for Vung Tau. They didn't know, however, that their working range included the entire province of Phuoc Tuy, where the Australian Task Force was, and most of the Rung Sat region. They'd answer any call from the Aussies, but it was the US Navy and Army that leant on them the most. There was plenty of dud ordnance around that had to be cleared away and destroyed. Or there was hazardous material that was out of date, suspect or had been mishandled. If a forklift operator skewered a 200-kilogram napalm bomb with the tongs, and gel started leaking all over the place, everyone would run for the hills and someone would call The Cave. Whenever the VC decided to rocket an airstrip or some other target, duds would be left lying around and given a wide berth until the Aussies came with their jeep and its sand-filled trailer to take the damned things away.

The threat of car bombs and booby-traps weighed on everyone's mind, especially US officers. If they left their car, or even their office, for too long, they'd be paranoid enough to call Team 3. It wasn't just that they feared their Vietnamese staff might have turned against them; some had just as much reason to fear their own men. Fragging – the murder of a soldier's superior – was an all-too-common death among US officers in South Vietnam. The divers helped investigate a suicide by grenade. Then there were even more out-there incidents, like the two GIs who tried to get high by eating C-4 explosive and ended up in comas. The divers' range of activity, in both a practical and geographic sense, was not defined. Given that commonly they would be sent on exchange to join an American EOD unit, they could and did end up operating throughout the whole of South Vietnam.

As more American officers became aware of what the divers could do, the more they factored them into their operations. The Australians relished the experiences, stepping up to meet all manner of challenges that they hadn't specifically been trained for. In the process, what Australian clearance diving was all about began to change. Instead of remaining focussed purely on maritime operations, dealing with ports and sea mines and covert beach surveys, they had to perform as EOD specialists on land and in shallow rivers. Just about every time the Yanks went into enemy territory they found ammo caches that needed to be blown up, bunker systems that needed to be destroyed and booby-traps that needed to be nullified, and they were pleased to find that the divers were extremely adept at such work.

From the second contingent onwards, the US Navy formally regarded the Australian unit as one of their own. First they were called Explosive Ordnance Disposal Mobile Unit Pacific (EODMUPAC) Team 21 and then later Team 35. The Australian commanding officers had to send weekly reports to the US Navy's EOD headquarters in Hawaii as well as their monthly reports to Canberra. Practically speaking, they were an American team that happened to made up of Australians. They were housed on an American base. They received US weapons, clothes and gear. When the phone rang, it was usually an American on the other end of the line. Their absorption into the US sphere of operations ultimately meant that most people in the Australian military had no idea what these men actually got up to in Vietnam.

From the outset the relief teams had their hands full. Even for well-trained professionals the learning curve was incredibly steep, and sometimes brutally so. The outgoing crew or 'short-timers' tended to pass the most dangerous jobs on to the new boys. With only a few days remaining on their deployment, they weren't prepared to take great risks. 'We're too short for that shit' was the common saying. The Americans preferred it that way, too – they considered short-timers bad luck. So this was why Lieutenant David Lees, commanding officer of the second contingent, and two of his men found themselves on special operations within hours of cracking their first beer in The Cave.

Lees, along with Petty Officer Bill Ellery and Able Seaman Jim Henry, joined a US-led harbour patrol that needed EOD support. The patrol was hunting down a Chinese trawler known to be smuggling weapons to the Viet Cong. When the trawler was found and challenged, her skipper refused to stop. The boat was fired upon and one shell triggered a powerful explosion on board. Much of the ammunition meant for the Viet Cong had blown up, but not all of it. Lees was tasked to lead the boarding party. The enemy vessel was now a lit powder keg and he had to step on board and look for any self-destruction charges that might have been laid. All up, Lees had been in Vietnam three days.

The handover period was an exchange of old stock for new. Just six months differentiated the two teams in terms of experience, but it seemed like a lifetime. Jeff Garrett was enjoying his first night in The Cave when two short-timers walked in. Petty Officer Robert Cox and Leading Seaman Dave Rhook looked like castaways. The pair had been called out to provide EOD support in an overnight operation down south. That was six days ago. Their clothes were filthy and their mood sombre, or maybe they were just bone weary. But they obviously had a story to tell.

As Garrett listened to the men's account his mind reeled. Cox and Rhook had gone with a task force on a sweeping operation up the Bo De River in the far south. It had followed a previous mission a few weeks earlier to rid the banks of numerous bunkers from which the Viet Cong had been harassing US patrol boats. Two divers had been on that mission, too. Chief Petty Officer Barry Wilson and Able Seaman

Harry Spicer had watched from the water as sections of the bank were napalmed for an hour. Then they had gone in and destroyed sixty-five bunkers and thirteen huts. They had also come across a concrete revetment that was duly demolished. The debris had barely settled from the blast when Wilson saw a member of his force freeze in his tracks and turn 'the colour of bad shit'. The man had put his foot on the trip-wire of a grenade booby-trap. Wilson disabled the device and the task force escaped without casualties. There had been no direct contact with the enemy but the raid must have infuriated the Viet Cong, for when Cox and Rhook went in on the follow-up operation, the reception was much hotter.

The force Cox and Rhook joined was made up of the tank-landing ship USS *Washtenaw County*, five patrol boats, two Huey Cobra gunships and forty Mike forces (troops of oppressed minorities like the Montagnards led by US Special Forces personnel). Their pay was supposedly anything they could plunder plus a wage. Unlike some of the South Vietnamese units, whose loyalty couldn't be counted on, the Mike forces were highly regarded soldiers.

The task force came under enemy fire a few times, which grew more intense as it moved upriver. The boats went as far as they could and then dropped off the men, who waded through tall reeds to reach firm land. The patrol was led by a sharp-eyed Cambodian scout, who was said to have once spotted a directional mine – one that sprays frag outwards in a limited arc – rigged to a tree from 300 metres away. Cox and Rhook followed behind the scout so that they could deal with any traps he found. Both Australians weren't too happy – they were days away from going home and here they were sneaking through the booby-trapped jungle and engaging in firefights. Over the six days they destroyed sixty-three bunkers, sixty-four huts, twenty-five sampans and a bridge. They collected twenty-two directional mines and forty-three grenades, some that still had wet paint on them, according to Rhook. They had to dig amongst a gravesite, looking for an ammo cache. Whatever enemy ammo they did find they blew up. On the last day, one of the boats radioed that it was sinking and under heavy fire from two VCs in a nearby bunker complex on the riverbank. The Mike force and the Australians landed and moved overland to attack the bunker from the flank and rear. Cox poked his head around an earth mound to get an eyeball on the bunker, and a spray of AK-47 bullets lifted the dirt twenty centimetres away.

What am I doing here? he wondered. *The relief team is in country – I'm too short!* A grenade was hurled into the bunker and the two VC were killed.

Rhook's account is bare-boned: 'We got sent in. We destroyed something like eighty bunkers. We had a few firefights. One American bloke got killed. He was sort of my partner on the job. He was standing in front of me when he got shot. The last afternoon was when we got in the real bad firefight. We were on the boat, then we went ashore and tried to come around from behind them, and that's what happened – we got 'em.

'Without being facetious, this is what we were trained to do. We were trained to do the unexpected and that's it. Something comes up, you've just got to handle it, that's it. It's a job and you do it. That's all. You'd come back, have a beer and didn't think twice about it.'

Still, that night in The Cave, the account held the new boy Garrett riveted. *Fuck me*, he said to himself. *We're in a war now. First day here and we're spinnin' warries. What's going to happen for the next six months I'm here?*

The answer was 'plenty'. By the time Garrett arrived, the ban on Team 3 participating in 'SEAL-type' operations had been lifted. Divers from all contingents had already been on many patrols not sanctioned by the navy. One incident, though, had the navy and Canberra in a state of alarm over what the divers were doing on the ground in Vietnam. In mid-March 1968, Petty Officer Ellery took part in a reconnaissance patrol to Long Son Island, a Viet Cong haven from which they sometimes launched rockets into Vung Tau. A fisherman stumbled across the patrol. That he was out after curfew made him a suspected VC collaborator, but then again fishermen had to make a living, and it was common for them to risk their lives to do so. Whatever the case, the man was seized. With Viet Cong known to be in the area, silence and the integrity of the patrol's cover was paramount. If the man was released, there was a great risk he would reveal the patrol's presence to the enemy. One of the SEALs took Ellery's knife and killed the fisherman. When details of the patrol and execution reached up top, the shit hit the fan. Contingent leader Lieutenant David Lees was strongly reminded that divers taking part in 'SEAL-type' operations were strictly forbidden. But the upward pressure for this to change did not go away.

In July the US Navy made three requests for the Australians to join night patrols into the Rung Sat. Navy SEAL advisors were taking a Vietnamese underwater demolition team in, and they asked the Aussies to take care of any booby-traps and help clear landing areas for future combat ops. This was an ally calling for active assistance in a war. Navy rules be damned: the divers were not about to sit in The Cave when they were needed on high-risk operations. But the patrol's task was not just to do prep work for future activity; it was to conduct ambushes on the Viet Cong and their 'tax collectors', the fund-raising squads that went around at night in their sampans, squeezing cash out of the locals.

Able Seaman Ray Cocks in Ellery's contingent went on the first patrol along with Lieutenant David Lees: 'At eleven o'clock at night we'd be landed on these islands – just mangrove-type stuff. We were strategically placed along the river's edge, and we sat there for about four or five hours and waited for these people to come along to ambush them.'

Nothing happened that night. The following night, Lees and Ellery were on patrol when nine sampans were seen approaching in the darkness. An ambush was quickly formed and, when the first sampan drew near, the patrol opened fire. Twenty-five Viet Cong were killed and two taken prisoner.

This event prompted Lees to lobby for an official change to the divers' mandate. In September 1968, Vice Admiral V. A. T. Smith, Chief of Naval Staff, paid a visit to the contingent that followed Lees'. It became clear to Smith that the official restrictions were hampering Team 3's ability to gain valuable on-the-job knowledge and experience. By joining these operations, the divers were in no more danger than the SAS. Smith wrote to General John Wilton, Chairman of the Australian Chiefs of Staff, advising that he was going to allow the divers to be employed on SEAL-type duties. Wilton himself then visited the team, and by January 1969 the change was official.

A month later Garrett's team arrived, led by Lieutenant Allan Davis. By this time the US Navy had formed a large riverine force to carry out Operation Game Warden, a shallow-water fleet that could patrol the waterways of the Mekong Delta. It was known as the 'Brown-Water Navy' and featured a vast array of craft, including mother ships, landing vessels and jet boats. The muscle of the riverine patrols were the Swift boats, 250 heavily armed PCFs (Patrol Craft, Fast). They had an M60 machine-gun in the cable locker up front, twin 50-cals in the middle and another gun fitted with a coaxial grenade launcher at the stern. On top of that, all crew and passengers had their own weapons. As they headed upriver they would pass jungle, mangroves and villages in turn, and it was all a free-fire zone – this was what the Yanks liked to call 'Marlboro Country', thick with natives, and anyone and anything from fig tree to farmer was fair game. And that's what they did, unloading on anything they even *thought* moved. They fired flare guns into the thatched huts to incinerate them, shot livestock, mortared gardens and fruit trees and lifted water buffalo off their feet with the 50-cal.

Garrett's first operation was a demolition job on 19 May 1969. He and Petty Officer John Brumley were tasked to destroy an enemy footbridge upriver, and four PCFs went along as protection. When they reached the bridge, Garrett got into the water with a few satchel charges. After he'd fixed the explosives, he swam to the riverbank. He was about to exit the water to tie another satchel charge to the bridge when a waft of rank body odour changed his mind. A bunker that had remained undetected from the boat was there to defend the bridge. Garrett swam quickly back to the boat, the patrol backed away, and the charges were detonated.

Garrett's patrol had done a fair amount of damage on the way up to the bridge, almost guaranteeing that on the way back they would take fire.

'They were a bit cranky after losing their houses, water buffalo and pigs,' he said. 'It was just a matter of when and where, not if.'

Garrett's boat was the first boat in the procession going up and the last going back. And, sure enough, they were ambushed.

'All hell broke lose. It was my first time under fire and I can remember everything basically being in slow motion. I saw something hit the water behind me and explode. Next thing I see the twin-50 gunner collapse. He was very badly injured, had his flak jacket open and the hole out the back wasn't real pleasant. I ended up taking over the M60 gun in the focsle and we did what you might call a token-gesture run of defiance back around, but the heart wasn't really in it. We had no idea where it came from but we were no more than fifteen metres from the shore when we took the ambush, so we were all pretty lucky.

'A rocket missed the boat by two feet right at the stern. I think they were probably aiming for the waterline and didn't allow for the time delay when you squeeze the trigger. The boat was going too fast, and it hit the water and exploded behind us. We took a bit of damage, but the other boats didn't take any because they were in front. We were the tail-end Charlie. They [the other boats] were a bit smarter.'

On that one patrol, Garrett's boat went through 6000 rounds of .50mm calibre, 4000 rounds of 7.62mm, 500 rounds of 5.56mm, 70 rounds of .81mm, 50 40mm grenades, 20 hand grenades and ten light anti-tank rockets. The American gunner died of his wounds.

In response to the riverine force raids, the Viet Cong began setting up barricades in the channels to impede and ambush the American boats. They would cut the ends of palm logs into tapered threads and screw them into the riverbed. Hundreds of these logs were lined up, standing vertical, criss-crossed and interlaced, tied together with barbed wire and often booby-trapped. From riverside bunkers hidden in the thick jungle, the VC would lie in wait, ready to ambush a stymied patrol.

Lieutenant Davis was shown aerial photos of the barricades and asked if they could be blown up. These particular ones were located in an extremely hostile area – previous raid attempts had been repelled when one boat was mined and another rocketed. Having decided that hose charges – lengths of explosive tubing – might do the job, Davis turned to his team for two volunteers. Chief Petty Officer Vick Rashleigh and Able Seaman Andy Sherlock soon found themselves in the muddy water inspecting a barricade for trip-wires and booby-traps while the security force spread over four boats provided suppression fire. They wove eight hose charges through the structure and the subsequent blast blew logs a hundred metres into the air.

≈

At one in the morning, four days after Garrett's bridge demolition, a call came through to The Cave. There had been a sapper attack down at De Long Pier and swimmers had been spotted in the water. John Brumley and Andy Sherlock were out searching ships, so it was Rashleigh, Garrett and Able Seaman Mick Ey who responded. They arrived at the pier to find that one swimmer had been captured. The hunt continued for others. There was a siren blaring, a lot of shouting, shots being fired, and the US military police were throwing hand grenades at just about any disturbance in the water. There had been many false alarms in the past, but this clearly was not. A new white rope could be seen running between the pier and the merchant ship *Heredia* – it appeared the enemy had successfully planted an explosive device.

About half an hour had passed between Team 3 taking the call and them standing on the pier directly over a possible mine. There was no telling whether the mine would be command detonated by a remote observer or whether it was timed. The divers had to do something quickly. Garrett, who had donned fins, mask and a scuba tank, jumped into the water. He had only had to follow the rope for about three metres before he came across a rectangular metal container the size of a kerosene tin.

'I went into a state of shock straightaway because I knew I was onto the real thing,' said Garrett.

He got straight out of the water and told Rashleigh that he'd found what he thought was a mine. At least that's what he tried to say.

'I could hardly talk, so great was the fear. I was trying to explain to Vic what it was, and he was like, "You alright? You alright?" Put it this way: I was terrified. I had problems getting the words out and he said, "Well, go down and have another look and see what you come up with."'

Garrett was only seconds into his attempted report when there was a dull explosion. With all the gunshots, grenades and scare charges going off in the vicinity, the men didn't take much notice.

Garrett re-entered the water. When he reached the device, he saw that the container had been ripped open – the mine had partially detonated. The forty pounds of explosive had been so poorly packed that most of the charge didn't fire. If the whole lot had blown, there is no doubt Team 3 would have lost three men there and then. Up top, Garrett reported his findings and Rashleigh sent Ey down for a second opinion. Ey confirmed Garrett's assessment and declared the mine was safe to haul up onto the wharf.

At around four o'clock a commotion erupted on the wharf and there was a fresh round of shooting. A second swimmer was hauled from the water just metres from where Garrett and Ey had been. He turned out to be a captain in the

North Vietnamese Army's 126th Sapper Regiment, but neither prisoner gave up any information about the devices. It was possible more had been planted. The divers continued to search the whole pier and every ship in the area.

At nine o'clock, Ey discovered a Russian BMP-2 limpet mine attached to a metal pylon on the wharf. He was able to ascertain that both safety pins were intact: the cutting-edge mine wasn't armed. On a second dive he saw the safety pin of the anti-removal device was also in place, so the mine was perfectly safe for him to wrench free by hand. When he surfaced clutching the mine, it took some convincing before the patrol boat crew allowed him to come aboard. There had been intel suggesting that the North Vietnamese had acquired this new Soviet mine, but up until now none had been discovered. In fact, this was the first time anyone in the Western world had laid hands on one. Yet while they were indeed being supplied some manufactured ordnance by their superpower backers, the Viet Cong and North Vietnamese mostly made their own.

On 28 June 1970, Team 3 members responded to another swimmer attack at De Long Pier. At two in the morning, the starboard bow sentry on the landing ship USS *Meeker County* spotted a suspicious nylon rope tied to the pier. Soon afterwards the sentry saw a man surface near the rope. He opened fire and the swimmer disappeared. Fifteen minutes later an unarmed sentry at the stern saw a swimmer twenty metres off to the port side and heading seaward. By the time grenades were thrown, the swimmer was beyond reach. The duty officer placed a call for EOD assistance at ten to three, and twenty-five minutes later three divers arrived. While Lieutenant Ross Blue went to speak with the ship's captain, Petty Officer John Kershler, who'd been part of Cuthbert's team and had returned to Vietnam four years later with the seventh contingent, and Able Seaman Jock Kingston inspected the rope.

'What they stupidly did was use new white nylon rope,' said Kershler. Anyone could tell the cord had not been in the water long. The rope extended from the pier and disappeared under the ship. 'I put some gear on and jumped in, followed the line and there it was.'

The mine was the size of a briefcase. It hung under the hull on the rope tied between the wharf and the port rudder. The mine carried around twenty kilos of plastic explosive. It had fishing floats fastened to the side to neutralise its buoyancy and make it easier to manoeuvre and position under water. An hour and ten minutes had elapsed since the first swimmer was spotted – a very uncomfortable length of time.

'You don't know how much time you've got,' said Kershler. 'But we had to do something. You couldn't say "there's something under there" and walk away from it. It was just a matter of, "Let's get it done."'

Kershler dived down and cut the mine free while an American boat crew took the port end of the line and towed the mine clear seaward, fixing it around a fishing stake far from any ship. Blue intended to give it twelve hours or so. If the mine hadn't detonated by then, they could haul it back up for examination. At around seven fifteen the mine blew, sending up a waterspout fifteen metres high. There was no doubt that if the mine had been left undetected it would have sunk the *Meeker County*. Kershler and Kingston continued to search all the other ships in the vicinity, as well conducting bottom searches for the bodies of the attackers. Nothing more was found, and the team returned to base just after ten.

In a letter of appreciation addressed to Blue, Vice Admiral Jerome H. King, Commander of US Naval Forces Vietnam, wrote, 'Although sufficient time had elapsed for the mine to detonate, you and your men unhesitatingly dived and successfully removed the mine ... The actions of the Royal Australian Navy Clearance Diving Team Three in this emergency bear testimony to outstanding professionalism and courage of the highest order.'

≈

Barry Bailey, who was a petty officer in the sixth team, was faced with an entirely different set of circumstances when called upon to deal with another mine. This weapon had been found by the residents of the village Phu Vinh in Tra Vinh province, located in the southern part of the delta. They'd fished it out of the river, taken it back to their village and left it in the village square for two or three weeks. Exposed to the elements, the device had baked in forty-degree heat by day and cooled overnight – a perfect way to destabilise explosives. Team 3 was called and Bailey and Leading Seaman Brian Bullock responded. They flew down and met with a US Special Forces advisor, who took them into the village. Countermining the object was not an option because the blast would flatten the village, and that wasn't going to win many hearts and minds.

'You had to strip it down,' said Bailey. 'I wasn't going to transport it with the detonator still in it, because that's the most sensitive part.

'It was hot and humid and sweat's pouring off us. I said to the Yank, "Get the villagers out of the way because if it goes off it's going to vaporise me, but it's gonna dig a big hole and spread stuff everywhere".'

Bailey checked for booby-traps. Typically, the VC would remove the pin from a grenade and plant it so that it would explode if disturbed. Thankfully, Bailey found no such surprise underneath. That was one less thing to worry about. The mine's metal casing was too hot to touch, so he splashed water over it.

'It was a beautiful piece of workmanship,' remembered Bailey. 'The seams were beautifully done. I got my drill out, drilled a little hole and had a look inside. There was a cavity. I gave it a tap; the charge was in the middle.'

On either side of the charge were buoyancy chambers to keep the mine suspended under water. It was command detonated: a wire would have been run from the mine into the jungle, and someone would have waited there to detonate it under a passing patrol boat.

No manuals existed for this job – this mine was a one-off. All Bailey had was training, knowledge and logic. Bullock stood at a safe distance as Bailey described each of his actions over a radio. 'So if "I'm going to cut the red wire" are my last words then he can put down, "Don't cut the red wire!"'

As he stared at the device, wondering how he was going to tackle it, Bailey's heart banged against his chest and his mouth became parched.

'All the years I've been trained, and I had to sit there and stare at it. I was thinking, *I want to go home!* Then I thought, *Well, you know, such is life. You've got a job to do. Do it.*'

Bailey took out his tin snips and started to cut the casing open. He was sweating profusely in the wretched humidity. The stench of a nearby open toilet hung under his nose in the still air. The villagers watched the lone foreigner impassively. Bailey suspected that they would have been happy to see him falter and get blown up with the mine. He kept working quietly and steadily until he was able to remove the detonator. It took him two hours to get to this point. Once this was done, though, the mine was safe. They put it into a jeep and drove further into the jungle. When they countermined the bomb if left a blast crater three metres deep by eight wide.

NINE
ON PATROL

ALEX DONALD WAS nearly forty when the first team went to Vietnam. As one contingent followed the other he wondered if the 'old boys' would ever get a run. Donald had been a sailor for fourteen years before being promoted from lower deck to lieutenant. As an officer he remained a very proud sailor, his white collar forever a little blue. With all his hands-on experience, he believed he was the man for the job in Vietnam, and ultimately his superiors thought the same.

'I clapped my heels and jumped for joy when they said, "You're going to run the sixth team",' he said, 'because there's nothing like doing it for real.'

For his first few weeks in Vung Tau, Donald followed procedure. He and his men did the nightly ship searches and typical EOD work. There were weapons and bodies to be retrieved from crashed aircraft, booby traps to tame and dodgy ordnance to dispose of. But Donald wasn't going to spend his whole tour waiting for the phone to ring, so he went out looking for work.

The Cave attracted many visitors and, with the volleyball court outside doubling as a helipad, chopper pilots counted among the regulars. One was Captain Robert Hoffman, a US Army pilot, who got on well with Donald. The Australian persuaded his new friend to fly him to every US Navy post in the delta. Donald was hell bent on making a publicity tour, promoting the expertise and versatility of his men to all and sundry. After these visits, the phone ran hot and the sixth contingent got busier than any team before it. In all, they clocked up seventeen special operations – barricade blasts, bunker demolitions, ambushes, reconnaissance patrols, sur-veillance, and search-and-destroys – a quarter of the total accrued by all eight contingents. Donald went on each and every one. 'I firmly believe you can't send your boys off to do something and not be there yourself,' he said. Ultimately, Donald was awarded the Distinguished Service Cross for 'cool, decisive leadership'.

'We were on the go,' remembered Barry Bailey with a laugh. 'At one stage there was only one of us left on the Hill.'

Once or twice a week, Donald would be in a US Army chopper doing aerial recons of hostile areas. He spent so much time in the air that Hoffman actually taught him to fly. Back on the ground he helped plan operations that involved his team.

In a typical bunker operation, three or four Swift boats

would head upriver carrying fifty-odd Vietnamese troops led by SEAL advisors. As with the barricade operations, or any canal patrols for that matter, the boats would run at full speed through narrow gauntlets of enemy territory. The troops and divers would lie on the afterdeck with guns cocked and aimed out, while the US Navy crew manned the mounted guns. There was no use looking for bunkers to shoot at because they were impossible to detect from the water; the only warning sign you would get from the enemy would be a muzzle flash. The place where no one wanted to stand was up in the driving bay, because that's where the Viet Cong tended to aim their first RPGs to try and cripple the boat. The crew took turns to drive. At the target area the troops would disembark and sweep up either side of the channel, raking the bunkers with bullets and checking for booby-traps. Once given the all-clear, the divers would go ashore with fifteen to twenty kilos of explosives in their backpacks. They'd then pull the igniter on the satchel charge and throw it into the bunkers as deeply as possible. These bunkers were strong enough to withstand air strikes unless hit directly, so the divers' job was to collapse the structure in on itself so that the whole thing had to be dug out again. They attached tear-gas bags to the charges so that crystals would disperse into the rubble and hamper the enemy's rebuilding efforts.

But that's not how it always worked. On one operation to clear a huge bunker complex the American advisor turned to Donald and told him there was an issue with the Vietnamese covering force – they were refusing to go into the area ahead of the divers because they knew it was booby-trapped.

When Donald asked how they were so sure, the American replied that half of them were VC and they put the traps there themselves. These men were part of the Regional Force, the name given to local militia assembled, armed and paid by the Americans in the hope that they'd defend their villages from the Viet Cong. As it turned out, many were keen to take the money while their loyalties, at best, remained split. On the whole, though, they did an adequate job of providing the Americans and Australians with security and local intelligence. Typically on these operations, there were also a couple of 'Kit Carson scouts', former Viet Cong who had surrendered under amnesty and changed sides. These scouts tended to be more reliable, but placing wholesale faith in any South Vietnamese troops was not wise. And on this occasion their first loyalty was to themselves, leaving Donald and Bailey with no choice but to advance with no protection at all.

'We had to go through and clear our own way into the bunkers and blow the shit out of them,' said Bailey.

Petty Officer John Kershler of the seventh contingent was quick to realise that it paid to keep a close eye on these scouts.

'You watched them because they know what's going on,' he said. 'You could watch their body language. Just the way they carried their rifle. Sometimes they'd just sling it over their shoulder and stroll along like it was a Sunday afternoon picnic. You knew you weren't going to get attacked. Other times they'd carry it properly and they were twitchy. And if they were all twitchy then you had to be on your toes. Anything could happen at any time.'

South Vietnamese troops were not just unreliable; they were sometimes hostile. Kershler experienced this first-hand when assigned to a large-scale EOD operation. Not long after arriving in Vietnam, Blue's seventh contingent was assigned to a massive, highly dangerous clean-up operation at a US base in Dong Ha, just a few kilometres south of the DMZ. The facility housed a large ammo dump containing around 18,000 tons of ordnance and was naturally a prime target for North Vietnamese artillery. The site came under heavy fire twice in 1968, with the loss of more than 8500 tons of ammo. When the smoke cleared, thousands of unexploded, partially exploded and damaged munitions were left scattered all over the ground. An initial clean-up effort resulted in two EOD personnel dead and eight wounded. The project was immediately put on hold, and for three years this vast mess of highly unstable ordnance was left to be baked by the sun and drenched by monsoons. Finally, a mini task force was formed to do the clean up by hand, combining EOD personnel from the US Marine Corps, Army, Navy and Air Force, plus members of Team 3. One by one, each round or shell or anti-personnel mine or grenade was carefully picked up and passed through a series of hands before being classified as safe and reusable or unsafe and to be destroyed. The men had to wear flak jackets and steel helmets in the searing heat. It was imperative that the men maintain absolute focus constantly, and so work continued in thirty-minute spells with ten minutes' rest in between.

'As if this wasn't bad enough,' said Kershler, 'bored ARVN [South Vietnamese] troops would take pot shots at us from time to time, despite threats of the most diabolical nature from the US Marine officer in charge of the operation.'

The job was completed in just over six weeks, during which ninety acres were cleared and 1025 tons of ordnance recovered or destroyed.

≈

On 14 August 1970, Team 3 spent their last day in Vung Tau. In mid-1968, newly elected President Nixon had released his 'Vietnamization' policy, a phased handover plan to pull the US out of what had become a festering, unpopular war, leaving South Vietnam to defend its own turf. As part of this process, Team 3's role in Operation Stable Door was taken over by two Vietnamese navy EOD teams. The divers had performed 7541 ship searches over their three and a half years in Vung Tau. During their preparations to leave, they stripped The Cave and donated the materials to a local orphanage. On 15 August, they relocated north to Da Nang, the main base in the northernmost military region in South Vietnam, I Corps.

Swimmers from the North Vietnamese 126 Sapper Regiment had posed a constant threat to shipping around Da Nang's port facilities. Unlike their Group 10 counterparts in the delta, the 126th Sappers weren't hampered by strong tidal currents. One of their swimmers was even found wearing an oxygen rebreather, an alarming find that showed they were capable of covert attacks. One hundred kilometres north, in the hotly contested Cua Viet River region near the DMZ, the

126th were wreaking havoc with an ingenious homemade weapon – the 'birdcage mine'. This was a pressure mine in which a football bladder, housed in a bamboo cage for protection, was fitted to an explosive charge. When sufficient pressure was applied by, say, an overpassing patrol boat, the mine detonated. Petty Officer Barry Wilson of the fourth contingent witnessed the destructive power of the birdcage mine firsthand.

Wilson had gone from Vung Tau to a base at Da Nang, and then to the mouth of the Cua Viet, having traded places with one of the US EOD team members. EOD units all over South Vietnam would swap personnel for two weeks here and there so that all teams got a better understanding of what was happening across the theatre.

'The northern side of the river was a free-fire zone,' said Wilson. 'We took incoming fire that first night. The next night we got called out at, I think, one o'clock in the morning with a report that a patrol boat had an unexploded rocket in its bow.

'We were given another boat to escort us upriver. We set out with the other boat in front of us. It came under fire from the shore. As we came around the corner we got fired upon. We increased speed and engaged the enemy. Shortly afterwards it [the front boat] got blown up. As soon as it increased speed, up it went and the whole lot of them, poor buggers, got killed. The boat looked as if a giant had picked it up and bent it.

'We stopped in the water – didn't move – and just floated around with the current until daylight came, and then we proceeded at a very slow speed back to where we came from. Later on I understood that these were countermeasures against the pressure mine. There may have been others in that area. The American lieutenant in command obviously knew things I knew nothing about. As soon as the other contact stopped he ordered our boat to stop immediately. I can assure you, just having the boat in front of you come under fire, and then nothing heard from them, and you're sitting out there in the bloody dark . . . Your mind wanders, mate.'

A couple of days after the incident Wilson's unit was sent back to retrieve the bodies. They'd been spotted from the air floating amongst the reeds. As expected, the enemy had booby-trapped the corpses, tying polystyrene boxes containing hand grenades to them.

'If we opened them, we'd have pulled the pin and triggered the mechanism,' said Wilson. 'We recovered them and blew [the grenades] up on the shore.'

In Da Nang, Team 3 didn't have to do hull and cable searches unless there was an emergency. They were kept busy performing routine EOD jobs and then occasionally being detached north to Cua Viet or fifteen kilometres south to Hoi An on missions that were far from routine.

Just inland from Hoi An was a large estuarine island called Cam Thahn. Being enemy territory, the island was a free-fire zone day and night. The US Marines' Jungle Surveillance Group (JSG) would often go ashore there to plant audio devices that allowed them to monitor Viet Cong troop movements from their receiving station in Hoi An. Some sensors would be positioned with Claymore anti-personnel mines which could be remotely detonated whenever a target came into range. Sometimes the mines would kill the enemy, other times a water buffalo. The JSG personnel also had to go and retrieve their gear from time to time. On any of these missions they wanted EOD specialists on hand to deal with any bunkers, booby-traps and ammunition stores they came across, and they asked the clearance divers to fill the role.

'Pretty much every time we went into that island there'd be shooting,' said Kershler. 'You can't tell if they're firing at you or someone else because in a jungle situation you can't see anyone. You just hear *choong! choong!* – the rounds flipping through the air. It's a bit disconcerting. And we're carrying all these explosives on us – plastic explosives and detonators. One bullet into that and there's nothing to take home. We'd just hit the ground and wait until everything had quietened down, then we'd get up and keep going.

'When the tide was out it was mud and reeds, then it was jungle. That was the hairy part: you're crossing this area of waist-deep water with no cover whatsoever, trying to keep everything dry. It was full of bomb craters. You'd be walking along and all of a sudden you'd be swimming, or at least trying to with boots and all the other rubbish we had on us. And once you got to the edge, that's where the booby-traps would start.'

The enemy were extremely skilled at using unexploded US ordnance to fashion deadly traps. Trip-wires were set to detonate a mortar or grenade dug into a shallow hole or tied to a tree. That wasn't the only way your own weapons could be used against you. When infiltration teams set up camp on the island, whoever was on watch spent long hours wondering, with every suspicious noise coming from the jungle, whether to fire the directional Claymore mines or not. He would also have to wonder if the sound was in fact the enemy turning the Claymores around.

'You had to stay switched-on all the time,' said Kershler. 'Then our guys would come in and stick the patrol boat into the mangroves, and you'd climb up a rope and get out. We'd do that at least once a week.'

By the time the eighth contingent arrived in Da Nang to relieve the seventh, Cam Thanh Island had cooled off. Few, if any, troops had been detected by the monitoring panel in Hoi An, and the Americans decided to retrieve the sensors. A small detachment was put together for the job and, purely because the area had once been very active, they decided they should take some EOD guys along. The job was described as a 'milk run', a light toe in the water for the incoming blokes and nothing too risky to spook the short-timers. Both teams sent a chief and one of the troops: John Dollar and John Aldenhoven from the old; John Gilchrist and Brian Furner from the new. They drove down to a village in Hoi An and met the US Army captain who was leading the operation. The rest of the party was made up of a few armed members of the JSG, a squad of US Army grunts and a Kit Carson scout – about twenty in all. They sped upriver, jumped into the shallows and waded to shore. The boats, crewed by South Vietnamese, promptly returned to base.

Able Seaman Furner, who was near the front, wasn't even

out of the water when the advance scout found a booby-trap on the track. A trip-wire stretched across the path was rigged to fire a US 105mm artillery shell into the victim. The Australians didn't bother fiddling with it. They pulled everyone back and countermined the shell. Their destination was only a few hundred metres ahead: a large clearing that had been so heavily bombed there was hardly any level ground left. The Viet Cong had built bunkers in amongst the craters, so this was where the surveillance team had planted their sensors. Given the low activity recorded recently, the Americans had expected to just walk in, grab their gear and leave. Now there was reason to think the mission would not go quite so smoothly.

With the booby-trap eliminated, the group moved forward, keeping a good distance between each other in single file. The divers were positioned not far behind the scout so they could deal with any more devices ahead of the rest of the patrol. When the group reached the clearing, the surveillance guys went for their sensors. One of them walked over to a crater filled with rainwater. Nearing the rim, he stepped on a pressure switch that detonated a 105mm US artillery shell beneath him. The blast took both his legs, but he was still alive. Furner and the other Australians were about twenty metres away.

'The shockwave blew us onto the ground,' said Furner. 'There was smoke and dust, and then all of a sudden we hear bloody AK-47 fire. There was a lot of noise – people yelling and carrying on – because it took us a few minutes to figure out where the firing was coming from.'

The medics rushed to the blast victim. The two soldiers nearest him were screaming that they had gone deaf. The others escaped with ringing in their ears. The medics put morphine into the victim and bandaged what was left of his legs. The incoming fire had continued, and now it was clear that it was coming from the wood line on the opposite side of the clearing. Furner and Leading Seaman Aldenhoven were ordered to join the medics.

'They got me and Mumbles to carry the bloke on a stretcher,' said Furner. 'I don't know why – maybe because we were young and fit. It was not heavy fire; it was sporadic. But it was heavy enough to get your attention, let me tell you.'

The American soldiers covered them as they put the fold-up stretcher together and lifted the victim onto it. They carried him back, and the whole group retreated to the protection of the bush. They retraced their steps to the river, Furner and Aldenhoven still carrying the stretcher, one of the soldiers who had gone deaf being helped along behind. Someone radioed for a Dust-off, the call sign for a medevac (medical evacuation), as the soldiers led the way to another clearing they knew where a chopper could land. When they reached this clearing, everything was quiet. The enemy had not given chase. Perhaps they had moved on.

At this point the soldiers realised that weapons belonging to two of the injured men and a radio had been left behind. The captain said he needed two people to go back and retrieve them – the radio in particular could not be allowed to fall into enemy hands. Despite there being several veteran soldiers in the group – the man who had trodden on the booby-trap had done eighteen months in country – Furner, an absolute fresher, and Aldenhoven put their hands up for the task. Well, sort of.

'Mumbles and I got volunteered by the chiefs,' said Furner. 'The two chiefs said, "Oh, these two will go." And when the chief told you to do something you did it, which is as good as volunteering.'

Furner and Aldenhoven returned to the cratered clearing. They were shot at as soon as they left the cover of the bush. They moved forward to the blast site by way of the fire-and-movement tactic, where one person maintains suppression fire while the other advances. Reaching the crater, they gathered up the weapons and the radio and covered each other back to the bush. All the while they were constantly mindful to stay on the track. This precaution was a golden rule before the incident, but all the more so now. There was something else to their aversion to falling victim to a booby-trap – for an EOD man, it would be quite an indignity to be blown to pieces by a device he never saw and never had a chance to beat. Furner had had two magazines taped together, each carrying thirty rounds. There were few left by the time they rejoined the group.

The Dust-off arrived soon afterwards, but enemy fire forced the pilot to pull away. Two hours later, a helicopter gunship came in, made two passes and 'brassed up' the wood line, allowing the medevac chopper to pick up the three wounded Americans. The man who had lost his legs died in the air.

The commanding officers of both the seventh and eighth contingents – Lieutenants Ross Blue and Jake Linton – recommended with equal weight that Furner and Aldenhoven be decorated for their actions. Unfortunately, the Australian Army headquarters in Saigon was willing to sign off on only one Distinguished Service Medal. Citations like these were not awarded purely on merit; a quota system that preserved scarcity and favoured rank took precedence. At any rate, army was not about to hand two DSMs from the quota over to navy. Since he was heading home, Aldenhoven got the DSM. Furner was told that he had the rest of his tour to earn a medal.

'If you want to dissect these operations, whether it be Long Thanh or whatever, there's always one bloke who stands out and then the group follows,' said Linton. 'I'm not saying they're not all brave and doing their duty and all the rest of it, but there's always one bloke who jumps in first, and Furner was that sort of a bloke.'

Until now, Furner had never given his account of the milk run and his role in the dramatic events. Over the years he has often heard the story told inaccurately and has only ever pointed out an aspect here or there that wasn't right or never happened.

'I don't really care,' he said about being deprived a medal. This is an attitude born of reason, not bitterness. Furner got on with the job while he was in the navy, and he got on with his life after he left. Besides, there were at least two other jobs he was involved in that he considered more dangerous.

Exactly a week after the milk run, the eighth contingent

took an emergency call from Harbour Security in Da Nang. The third typhoon in the space of a month had wrenched an ammunition barge from its mooring in the harbour and it had run aground on a sandbank just offshore from a village. The reason this constituted an emergency was that a small but intense fire had broken out on the barge's deck. Essentially, the barge was now a 150-ton bomb with a lit fuse. Harbour Security staff weren't going to go anywhere near the thing. Chock-full of high explosives – 81mm mortar bombs, 175mm artillery projectiles, 66mm anti-tank rockets, 70mm rockets and whatever else – this was a job for those Australians. This was still the handover period and members of the seventh contingent declined to go. They were 'too short' for such a risky job, so the three able seamen newcomers – Tony Ey, Larry Digney and Furner – piled into the team jeep and headed down to the harbour. They were told there was an outboard skimmer boat waiting for them at the Harbour Security wharf.

Ey was at the wheel. Once they were underway they realised they had a problem – none of them knew the way to the wharf. Ey made a couple of wrong turns, wasting precious minutes. Eventually they reached Harbour Security and were shown to their boat.

'You could see the barge out in the bay,' said Ey, 'and the intensity of the fire, to our eye, meant that explosives were burning. We thought, *Oh shit. It's not a good thing to go out there*. But what do you do? It's your job. You don't let it burn. There's high explosives out there. You've got to go and have a look.

'So the three of us jumped in the skimmer. We opened the throttle, turned towards the barge and as we began to plane the whole thing went *kabooom*. Just detonated. It was like a nuclear blast. Mushroom cloud. There were pallets and shit going everywhere, flying over our head.'

In fact, the barge only partially detonated. Half the pay-load – seventy-five tons – went up in one monumental blast that all but flattened everything on the shoreline and sent a violent shockwave through Da Nang. The remaining seventy-five tons of ammunition had been scattered 300 metres in every direction. It didn't take long for Ey, Digney and Furner to realise that if they hadn't lost their way, or if a member of the old crew who knew the way had tagged along, they would have been on that barge. The eighth contingent would have lost three divers within days of arriving in Vietnam.

The members of Team 3 then had a huge clean-up job on their hands, retrieving all the scattered ordnance from the harbour depths and surrounds. They were still at it four months later.

'Initially, we were most cautious,' said Linton. 'But the sheer magnitude of the task caused a gradual degradation of our attention to detail. I have vivid memories of a line of our team members and children down to toddlers all carrying damaged and potentially dangerous ordnance and loading it into our vehicle. We then transported these items through the city to the demolition site. Marvellous how much differ-ence the war made to the interpretation of regulations.'

In the following months, the eighth contingent responded to six more ammo barge emergencies.

The other job Furner considered more dangerous than his Cam Thanh Island heroics happened in November, when a thirty-five-metre US Navy utility vessel was caught in yet another typhoon and capsized. With all twelve members of the American crew missing and 150 tons worth of ammunition – 105mm and 81mm white phosphorous rounds – in the hold, the vessel washed onto a beach near Hue, to the north of Da Nang. A salvage operation was launched with Linton in command. Four Australians, a US Navy salvage team and a few US Army divers were dispatched by Chinook to get the operation started.

One look at the wreck and it was clear that retrieving the bodies and ammunition was going to be extremely difficult. They decided to try and right the vessel using three offshore tugs. To do this, the divers had to first attach heavy lines to the wreck. In the heavy surf and longshore current, they were smashed repeatedly against the stern. The lines were eventually fixed, but the rough seas made the operation too perilous for the tugs. In the end, they cut through the hull and the divers went in to search the hold. No bodies were found. The ordnance was retrieved but after two weeks the conditions had not improved, and so the wreck was left to rust.

Throughout the operation the party had had to camp at the site. They were fired on initially but, according to Furner, that was nothing compared to the treacherous nature of the job. Either way, they were happy to pack up and head back to Da Nang.

≈

On 19 April 1970, the eighth contingent handed over duties to a US Army EOD team. All the EOD needs of Dong Ha and the entire I Corps region were to be taken up by two US and three Vietnamese personnel. This kind of baton dropping, so common throughout the Vietnamization program, made it hard for the likes of Linton to close the door on the job with unqualified satisfaction. 'It was as if no one really cared whether we'd been there or not,' he said.

The lack of resolution affected divers, as it did other Vietnam vets, in more powerful ways and for decades to follow. Members of the eighth contingent were among the first Australian servicemen withdrawn from Vietnam. Regardless of whether they had wanted in or were forced in, they had left to serve their country. They boarded the Qantas charter, nicknamed 'the Freedom Bird', happy to be alive and homeward bound at last. But they were as ill-prepared for home as they were for the war. To what measure Australia's shameful welcome compounded the debilitating effects of their war experience depended on the individual.

'Every bloke who served in Vietnam thought we did a hell of a good job,' said Tony Ey. 'We came home hoping, sort of half-expecting, to be treated like a returning veteran who's served his country. We were very aware of the World War II vets, the Korean War vets – they came home as heroes, they had parades, they couldn't buy a beer in a pub.

'I came home on a Qantas flight and it arrived after curfew in Sydney. They didn't want anybody to see us come in. We felt like criminals being sneaked into the prison at night. Then it was, "Pack your bags, boy. Here's your leave pass.

Piss off. That's your posting in two weeks." Never mentioned again. I think that hurt a lot of blokes, that we were treated like shit. Fortunately, that's mostly gone now. But, you know, it plays with your head a bit.'

Trying to re-engage with civilian life was often a surreal experience. Blokes were still in their early twenties when they returned. They went to parties and no one spoke about Vietnam. If someone asked, it was best that they denied ever going because it wasn't worth the hassle. Saying you were a Vietnam vet wasn't ever going to get you laid. Young women in particular despised you. And just as puzzling and disturbing as the scorn were the stunning displays of apathy, as though to present a benign indifference to the war was somehow proper.

Tony Ey had had a bizarre taste of this when he came home mid-tour for a week's R & R. The night he arrived in Sydney he went out for dinner at Doyle's restaurant in Watsons Bay. Ey's fiancée was there, as was his brother Mick, who had served with the fifth contingent, and his wife. Making up the table were two other diver mates who hadn't been to Vietnam. During the course of the evening no one mentioned Vietnam or the war once. No one even asked Ey how he felt – whether it was good to be home, whether he wanted to go back. Not even his brother.

'Twenty-four hours out of a war zone and you're going back in several days, and life's just normal back here. It was hard to deal with.'

Once their leave was up and they resumed normal duties as a diver, the experience of the veterans was mixed. It would be fair to say that many divers who hadn't gone were jealous of those who had. While some returnees were never asked about their experience, others were queried openly. Maybe it depended on age and rank. Perhaps those who felt most envious were the younger men.

Despite the lack of formal recognition or welcome home from the Australian Navy, what the members of all Team 3 contingents did in Vietnam began to permeate the branch. The role of the clearance diver was never going to be the same. From those teams a transformation started that was almost unthinkable before the Vietnam War: clearance divers weren't just sailors anymore.

'It all changed after Vietnam,' said Kershler, who began instructing upon his return home. 'It was not just about jumping into the water; it was about weapons, booby-traps and munitions. You have to be part army, to think like a soldier; not a sailor sitting on a ship.'

After four years spent in the Vietnam War, the soldiering gene had become a vital part of a clearance diver's overall make-up. No longer a thing wholly of the sea, the diver had become amphibious.

≈

In the early 70s, the US Navy awarded two Navy Unit Commendations to Team 3 in recognition of their outstanding courage. The paperwork was received by senior Australian naval staff and for some reason they took no action whatsoever to officially recognise, accept and honour the awards.

The commendations sat in a filing cabinet somewhere until someone stumbled across them almost forty years later.

The Australian Chief of Navy at the time, Russ Crane, put his weight behind giving the members of Team 3 their due and, on 1 October 2010, forty-three vets and the families of those deceased were honoured by Crane and Admiral Gary Roughhead, no less than the US Navy's top dog. The ceremony took place by the water at HMAS *Waterhen* and, while the figures of those men were not as lean as they once were, they walked lighter on their feet. They had always felt they had punched above their weight and, while the Americans had paid them due recognition, their own country hadn't until now. It was as though Australia had finally taken pride in what these men had done so many years ago.

TEN
RUNNING WITH THE SAS

In FEBRUARY 1978, a bomb explosion outside the Sydney Hilton snapped Australia out of its docile attitude towards terrorism. Inside the hotel were a dozen VIP guests: Prime Minister Malcolm Fraser and eleven other state leaders, gathered for a Commonwealth Heads of Government Meeting. Two garbage collectors and a policeman died in the blast, but the message was political. Citizens may have been alarmed, but politicians were terrified. All of a sudden 'no-worries' Australia seemed a great place to stage an assassination. Investigations into the bombing lacked resolve – not even the explosive used was determined – but the government's response did not. Fraser ordered a complete overhaul of Australia's domestic security net. A key element of this initiative was the creation of the nation's first counterterrorism assault squad.

In the April 1979 Cabinet paper that proposed raising this specialist force, it was conceded that Australia had been slow on the uptake. Terrorism had surged in the 1970s, its coming of age studded with grim landmarks: the Munich Olympics massacre, the body thrown from a Lufthansa plane in Athens, the airport sieges at Entebbe and Mogadishu. But the extremists were feeding on politicians as well as passenger jets. A month after the Hilton bombing, the Italian Prime Minister, Aldo Moro, was kidnapped and later murdered. Adolph Dubs, the US ambassador to Afghanistan, met the same fate. All over the world, militant groups like the PLO, Baader-Meinhoff and the Red Brigades saw violence as a valid demand lever and bystanders as blood collateral. And just before the decade was out, Iranian extremists overran the US embassy in Tehran and Islamic terrorists seized the Grand Mosque. Events like these prompted Britain (who, of course, had the IRA to contend with), America, the Netherlands and West Germany to stand up counterterrorist commando squads. It took the Hilton bombing and a weird little Hindu sect called Ananda Marga to push Australia down the same path. Whether or not the sect's members actually carried out the Hilton bombing didn't really matter – the government couldn't help but respond. And whether guilty or not on this count, the Ananda Marga's nasty rap sheet and ASIO case file had convinced the Fraser government that they were not just cranky hippies but haywire revolutionaries. Australia simply had no way to prevent or deal with premeditated acts of cause violence. Clearly, this had to change.

The counterterrorist job was assigned to the army's

Special Air Service Regiment. These ultra-disciplined soldiers were covert specialists, ghost troops who could move
unseen behind enemy lines and live off bugs. But if the need
arose they could go the full commando and throw down an
offensive raid – all blunt force, precision fire and noise – better than most. The Regiment, as the SAS is commonly
referred to in the Australian military, made one of its three
squadrons a counterterrorism unit and began training their
men in hostage recovery. The inaugural team had only been
training a month when they were given a real-life practical
demonstration of their job.

On 30 April 1980, six Arab separatists overran the Iranian
embassy in London. Following a few days of negotiations,
a hostage was killed. Britain's course of action changed at
once: Operation Nimrod was immediately given the go-
ahead. The civil crisis was now a military operation and the
British SAS was let off the chain. On 5 May, as the stand-
off was beamed live around the world, millions of viewers
saw several dark avengers appear on their television screens.
With commercial aircraft flying lower to increase ambient
noise, they rappelled down the white townhouse walls and
blew open the windows with frame charges before storming
inside. When the dust had settled on the fifteen-minute raid,
five of the six terrorists had been shot dead. One hostage was
also killed, but nineteen others were rescued. In preceding
years, Israeli and German commandoes had staged equally
stunning and successful operations to free hostages from
terrorists, but it was the SAS storming of Princes Gate that
really put counterterrorism on the map. Britain basked in

reflected glory – a hard-nosed, ballsy kudos – that to some extent came at the expense of America, who had failed to free her own embassy hostages still being held captive in Iran at the time. At any rate, Fraser would have been able to point at those black storm troopers on the box and say, 'That's what we've got.' Or, at least, 'That's what we've ordered.'

In May 1980, the Regiment's counterterrorism squadron became operational. At the same time, Britain's newest counterterrorism unit, formed by the Royal Marines, did likewise. The Comacchio Company was a 300-strong force raised to guard Britain's nuclear arsenal and to retake offshore assets, like oil rigs and ships, if seized by terrorists. This latter capability was also desired by the Australian government. What would the SAS do if a Bass Strait oil platform was captured? They could parachute onto the rig – no problem – but chances are they would be spotted and the alarmed enemy might turn the platform into the world's biggest barbecue. At the very least a maritime counterterrorism force needed to be able to execute beyond-horizon, clandestine infiltrations. This required a degree of dive knowledge and boat skills the SAS simply didn't have. Only one group within the Australian Defence Force did: the Navy's clearance divers. So it was decided that navy divers would provide the basis for a thirty-man water troop within the new squadron. Since counterterrorism was entirely the Regiment's gig, they would run selection, training, qualification, gear and weaponry out of Campbell Barracks, their base in Swanbourne, Perth. The clearance diving branch would feed them candidates from Sydney.

On paper, this was a logical and fair arrangement. On the ground, it was a little more complicated. Various elements within the Regiment resented having to accommodate, train and operate with a bunch of sailors. This was more than inter-service rivalry. The Regiment doesn't 'do' guests. There was no better special forces outfit in the world. No one could just rock up and expect to keep pace, and they certainly weren't inclined to be slowed down by anyone. Yet here they were being told to billet sailors. As far as the SAS was concerned, there were only two things worth knowing about clearance divers: they weren't special forces and they weren't army. Whatever brand of hell they'd been though to win their own tribe's colours didn't matter. The Regiment would have simply preferred to raise their own water capability from scratch and keep it all in-house. But that's not what the Fraser government wanted. The Regiment had to play ball, end of story. And so the two most elite military outfits in the country were set on a collision course.

In mid-1980 an SAS interview panel flew to Sydney to screen the branch's candidates. If the SAS had to take divers then it was going to pick which divers got to undertake their rigorous selection trial in Perth. For the first rotation, they decided to take a commanding officer, a warrant officer, a chief, a petty officer and ten or so sailors. All the candidates faced an SAS colonel, regimental sergeant major and a shrink. Commander Clem Littleton, a veteran clearance diver, sat alongside them.

'It was almost like a formal court,' remembered Larry Digney, who was interviewed for the position of chief. 'There was a table with these guys sitting on one side and the interviewee sitting on the other being grilled. Questions were coming from different angles, and you just answered.'

One of the first to be interviewed was Warrant Officer Phil Narramore. He had been skippering a boat down at HMAS *Creswell* in Jervis Bay when the call came through for volunteers to take counterterrorism (CT) training. Sick of driving his boat, Narramore put his hand up and travelled to Sydney for the physical and interview.

'They asked me all these stupid questions and one was, "When did you last have a fight?" And I said, "I haven't had one since Saturday." They virtually dropped their pens.'

The panel asked Narramore to elaborate. He explained that on Anzac Day he had stood up for a young sailor who was copping verbal abuse from a civilian in an RSL. Narramore said he told the man to leave the sailor alone. A mouthful of abuse was directed at Narramore, and the two men ended up fighting. The panel questioned whether this was the kind of example a warrant officer should be setting. Narramore assured them that no one had seen the fight: he had followed the bloke into the toilets and taken care of him there. The panel moved onto the next question. Later, Narramore was told he had been selected as the warrant officer, the second-in-charge of the divers bound for Perth.

The chosen divers had three months before they were due to head west and immediately launched into intensive training.

'We were the fittest guys in this country,' said Narramore. 'We had our own physical training instructor. We were running nine-mile runs in under ninety mins with full pack – then we'd go back to *Penguin*, jump in the water at six o'clock at night and swim to Manly. That would be two hours. You'd get out alongside the wharf where the restaurant was, smell the fish and chips cooking, then get straight back in the water. Two hours back. This went on day in, day out. Rifle range, running, jumping, shooting – doing all this sort of crap for three months. When we arrived at Swanbourne we were really top notch. We were ready to go.'

In Perth, the divers were put through a modified version of the SAS selection test, the infamous Cadre course. They all passed. When CT training started, though, it was a different story.

'They just really didn't want us there,' said Narramore. 'They absolutely hated us. They gave us a dreadful time. They found ways to get rid of guys.'

The training was high-pressured, intense stuff. It had to be. And the fundamental requirement of a CT squadron member was to be an accurate and judicious shot. The acid test for this was close-quarters battle training – learning how to storm into rooms and put double taps into the foreheads of bad guys. And if only because they weren't soldiers who practically had a firearm grafted to their bodies, the divers were generally short on weapons awareness. In this constrained environment they had to learn how to handle a weapon, how to not 'laser' (inadvertently point weapon at) people and how to kill the right target in the dark through a gas mask – and fast. One by one the divers were failed. Weapons safety breaches mainly, but there was a variety of dubious, or at best subjective, infringements: technical, psychological and personal. Too aggressive. Too timid. Too immature. Too weapons illiterate. The way the divers saw it, they were simply being culled. The respect factor was zero. Thirty-something senior divers, men who had served in Vietnam, would have some Corporal Raw-Bones screaming in their faces something about navy pussies not knowing butt from barrel. Of the twenty-odd divers in the first batch, all but four were failed at the CT training stage. There was a similar failure rate with the next rotation. This was unquestionably a slap in the face for navy. Their can-do, triple-A-rated operators were supposedly duds in the counterterrorism department.

Phil Narramore was among the few who passed CT training, but he had no desire to stay on at Swanbourne and be treated like dirt, taking orders from lesser rank. He returned to *Penguin* and helped train Perth-bound candidates. On occasion, the role took him back to Swanbourne with his boss, Commander Littleton. It was on one such visit that he got into a fight – and not just any old punch-up. This was an epic encounter that divers and soldiers still talk about decades later.

Littleton and Narramore had had a couple of beers in the sergeant's mess before the commander left to visit relatives off base. Having been lodged at the mess, Narramore remained behind. He went and joined half a dozen SAS troopers. It didn't take long for the mood to sour.

'One of them, a sergeant he was, started putting shit on the navy,' said Narramore.

Now, Narramore had had to bite his tongue on many

occasions over at Swanbourne. He knew he was on Regiment turf, but throughout his career most servicemen he knew had abided by a fundamental respect for ranks across defence. If air force or army guys were in his mess, as a warrant officer he made sure they were looked after. He saw that the RSMs at Swanbourne were treated like gods – and he was senior to them. He didn't expect grovelling, just the recognition he was due. This particular sergeant showed how much respect he had for Narramore by knocking him off his stool.

'I got up and said, "You've got two choices – the car park or I'm going to have you run in for striking a senior officer." So he said, "The car park."'

The two men walked out, trailed by an excited entourage. From there, they set upon each other like pit bulls. The money you could have made off this fight. In years to come, this car-park stoush became rich fodder for legend and myth. The two combatants were not mere individuals; they were champions of their kin, like the old single-combat warriors shoved forth by their tribe to spare the untold bloodshed of full-blown war. The grudge in this match ran deeper than Army versus Navy; this was SAS Trooper versus Clearance Diver.

Both their faces were broken and bloodied. Their skin was torn up by the gravel they wrestled upon. If not for the ring of cars parked around them, they may well have rolled out of Swanbourne and pummelled their way across the Nullarbor. The onlookers cheered, even as their own cars buckled under the punishment – no one would stop this for the world. In the end, both combatants had had enough. There was no winner and no loser, and that was somehow fitting. For years to come, trooper and diver alike spoke of 'the fight', mainly because it was an epic. For the sailors, though, what really stirred their pride was the fact that Narramore had stuck up for navy in the heart of SAS territory.

'The plate in my front tooth was broken,' said Narramore. 'I was a mess. The next morning I fronted up, and I thought Clem [Littleton] was going to kill me because he was a bit of a hard-arse. He walks in and says, "*What the fuck happened to you?*" I had gravel cuts all over me. We'd both done quite a job on one another.'

A week later, Littleton received photos of the damage to the cars. The Regiment wanted Narramore to pay half the damage. Littleton then took a telephone call from Swanbourne.

'I was on the phone when they rang,' said Narramore, 'and he said, "He's not paying nothing!" and slammed the phone down. About a month later the SAS colonel and RSM came over, and I had to spend a day with them. I took the RSM up for a beer, but the issue was never raised again.'

About the only outcome of lasting consequence was that no more divers of Narramore's rank were sent over again. Some divers say the fight ultimately meant nothing, but many, like Larry Digney, claim differently.

'What it did was level the playing field a bit,' said Digney. 'We stand very firmly behind our motto, *United and undaunted*, and I think that showed we hold our ground. The level of animosity was sustained, but the level of respect changed.'

There were many reasons an SAS trooper or NCO might

resent the navy intrusion. One was the fact that counter-terrorism was a cash cow. The Regiment received generous CT funding, and no politician would dream of skimping on it since they were the most likely beneficiaries. The Regiment did not want to cede any CT capability to the dive branch. Most commonly, though, the enmity stemmed from the fact that the first rounds of divers didn't do the full Cadre course – they were put through a filleted version.

This modified course was designed by SAS specifically for the divers, and some say it was harder than the original. Regardless, it was seen as being diluted, and if you hadn't passed the full Cadre course, you simply hadn't proven yourself.

In 1985, the Regiment began putting divers through the Cadre course proper. About twenty divers lined up along-side about 150 soldiers. Not only did every fit diver finish the course, but the majority passed CT training and were accepted by the Regiment. If that wasn't an emphatic enough statement of worth, in 1985 and 1986 clearance divers *topped* the Cadre course.

While the divers' initial high failure rate had been insult-ing, they didn't sit around in Sydney scratching their heads. They got smarter. Running around with a backpack full of bricks didn't teach you field craft. Doing shuffle runs up Mosman's steep Awaba Street in army boots – up to the first cross street, back down to the boulevard, up to the next cross street, back down and so on until the 500-metre crest was reached – may well have built strength of character, but it didn't build soldiering skills.

'We spent ten weeks with 1 Commando Company up in Georges Heights,' remembered Paul Darcey, who had trialled in 1981 and, like the majority of his group, failed. 'SAS instructors came over and we learned navigational skills, bush skills, patrolling skills. Then we'd do the two- to three-week parachuting course, then fly over to the west where they put us through the mill for another three or four weeks. The younger [army] guys, the ones we were doing courses with, were fine. The older guys – warrant officers and sergeants who'd done Vietnam time – there was no way in the world they wanted friggin' matlows [sailors] getting involved in their closed SAS shop.'

Commander Pete Tedman was a petty officer when he went to Perth. The SAS put him on the selection course so he could report back to navy whether or not the divers were getting stitched up.

'I saw why they could get away with failing everybody,' said Tedman. 'There were lots of activities during the selection. At the end of the day you'd come together and have all the selectees' files with a photo. They'd hold up a photo and if anyone in that room said "No" – and there was no real justification required because the selection group was ultimately trusted by the CO – you were off course. Simple as that.'

'I've seen CDs pushed to the absolute limit on that course, where they nearly drowned,' said Karl Price, who successfully qualified in 1988. 'The same with some army guys, but I think some of the [navy] guys' faces didn't fit and they sure as hell tried their best to break you. That's the reality of the selection course: if you show weakness, they'll home in on you and they'll try to break you. If you pass everything and come out shining and they still don't like you, they won't take you. If your face doesn't fit, you're stuffed.'

That being said, it wasn't lost on some divers that their own organisation, at least in years gone by, could be just as subjective. Cross the wrong supervisor and you could be doing push-ups until you collapsed and then be kicked out for being a wimp. Hand the same guy a freshly speared snapper every now and then and you were good as gold. There were the official tests, and then there was the 'good bloke, right temperament' test. Many a good diver never made it into the branch simply because his face didn't fit.

The Regiment's attitude towards divers changed very quickly once they were put through the full Cadre course. Many divers detected no hostility whatsoever. Tim Hayes had just turned twenty when he 'volunteered' to go west in 1986. 'I got the call to go to *Penguin*, walked into the dive school and the warrant officer at the time, champion guy, said to us, "You guys are all volunteers for this: if you're not a volunteer, you can hand in your right-arm rate." So we were all volunteers. I was pretty happy at the time. Life was good and I didn't really need it, but I thought I'd do it anyway.'

Hayes headed west to take the Cadre course with about 170 other hopefuls. Names were called out and men were dispatched in ten-man patrols. Hayes's name was never called. He was the last man standing, a kid left facing a few SAS heavies. He was humbled to be in their presence – make that terrified. They sent him away to register, and he presented himself to a corporal. He was so nervous his knees were shaking.

'You a matlow, are ya?'

'Yes, corporal.'

'Good. We need you matlows.'

That corporal never knew how much Hayes appreciated those words. From that point on he never experienced or witnessed any kind of prejudicial treatment of divers. There was the occasional good-natured dig, but to his mind it was a completely level playing field.

Hayes had been exceptionally well prepared, having been put through hell by older divers before arriving in Perth. Nothing was given away – he had to learn and earn every bit of his work-up training – weapons, navigation, etc. And he knew you had to be grey. Always do your best, but be grey. Don't be loud. Don't laugh or it will be read as you laughing at the DS, the directing staff. After completing his Cadre course and transferring to Campbell Barracks, Hayes was told by his DS that he'd topped the entire course. There was no formal record of this because the 'student of merit' award was handed out when the newly qualified SAS troopers graduate and received their coveted sandy berets. In 1988, Hayes won the annual triathlon (which was actually a biathlon that year) that is staged during Regimental Birthday Week. Another diver, Petty Officer Rod Allchurch, won the over-30s event.

'When we got the trophies from the CO of the Regiment, he said to us, "I bet you navy lads love nothing better than coming over and kicking the army's arse." I said, "You got that right, sir." And that was all in good fun. It was a joke,' said Hayes. He also found it amusing that the spaces for the 1988 winners on the trophies were left blank. On Anzac Day that same year, it was Hayes who laid the wreath at the memorial in Campbell Barracks, an honour reserved for the youngest trooper in the squadron.

'There you go,' said Hayes. 'What's a navy guy doing laying a wreath at something so significant? That's total acceptance.'

A year after Hayes did his selection course, a Special Duties Unit was established at HMAS *Stirling* as part of Team 4, the divers' Perth-based operational outfit. All CT candidates went there for pre-course prep. The training was run by divers who had been on line in the CT squadron, and they proceeded to build and maintain a near-perfect pass rate on SAS selection.

It's worth noting that in 1988 the navy went beyond the clearance diving branch to recruit volunteers to try out for counterterrorism selection. Maybe the branch couldn't cope with the Regiment burning through so many divers, so the navy opened the door to all trades: cooks, engineers, pilots, anyone. Some sixty men made it through vetting but, after being put through the scuba air and oxygen rebreather course, only around fifteen headed west for the pre-selection work-up.

'I take my hat off to those guys,' said Karl Price. 'Very few other than professional soldiers ever attempt the Cadre course, let alone sailors. Unfortunately, for nearly all who completed the course, their faces didn't fit. They were deemed immature, not suitable. I recall a comment from the

DS: "We don't want them. We only want clearance divers. You guys know what it's about."'

For those clearance divers being groomed for selection, failure was not an option. No one wanted to let the branch down. A case in point was Dave Pearsall, who passed in 1988. Before leaving *Penguin* he was confidently informed by a diver who had failed the Cadre course that he didn't have what it takes. Pearsall's mother died while he was on work-up training in Perth. He returned to Sydney, saw his mother to her grave, went back to Perth, finished the work-up, passed the Cadre course, passed the training and went on line.

'The only thing worse than failing the Cadre course would have been to face the diving branch afterwards,' he said. 'Pride in your unit isn't restricted to the SAS.' In twenty-eight days, Pearsall's weight dropped from eighty-three kilograms to sixty-nine.

'If you were going to do the Cadre course, you didn't fail,' said John Isles, who qualified as a sniper for the CT squadron in the early 90s. 'No one had physically failed. The only failures were by physical injury. No one had ever pulled the pin.'

What soldiers would have given to be able to attend an organised, tailored program like the divers. For these guys, making the SAS meant absolutely everything. Undertaking the Cadre course was the critical point of their military career. There could be no greater testament of character than to wear the sandy beret. The divers, on the other hand, had already been accepted into their dream role. Joining the Regiment was a secondment, not a career. If they'd wanted to be SAS, they would have joined the army.

One of the Special Duties Unit's first aims was to get the divers' endurance up, because that's what the Cadre course was – a three- to four-week endurance test. So they were sent out on twenty-kilometre pack marches. Initially it was 'clean fatigue', then extra weight, like battle armour and pack, was added. Staying on your feet became the top priority. At the Regiment, if you didn't march you were off course.

'Your feet would be aching,' said Isles. 'More weight meant more blisters, deep blisters. We had people on the side of the road with blood blisters inside their feet, subdermal. We knew we had to march again the next day, so we'd cut two small holes in the blister and inject Medaphene, which is like alcohol, straight into the blister. The pus would come out, the alcohol would go in, stinging like all buggery. You'd take the pain and carry on. Twenty minutes later that skin is dry and sealed, and you're good to go marching again.'

Morning runs would go for hours through sand dunes or along the beach and into the shallows to trudge through thigh-deep water thick with seaweed. They rested doing push-ups. Then they would learn how to strip and assemble a weapon, how to handle it and how to not laser people. There were radio procedures, day–night navigation lessons through the *Stirling* Range and then across the featureless dunes of Lancelin where you had to pace count and use dead reckoning.

The divers became outstanding performers, not just in the SAS selection course, but in the CT training as well. When it came to shooting, close-quarters combat (CQB), sniping and assaulting, the navy was at the very least holding their own, and often setting the pace. The credibility stock of navy within the Regiment rose accordingly.

For some, though, this wasn't enough. Whatever lingering resentment that existed stemmed mostly from the fact that the divers were getting fast-tracked into the Regiment's cream job at the time: counterterrorism. Once they had done the selection course and the parachute course, the divers could go straight into CT training. This put them at the same level as a fully qualified SAS soldier, who after selection had spent a year doing 'green' training – the core SAS competencies of moving through the bush, escape and evasion, and covert reconnaissance – to be qualified to wear the sandy beret. Because they hadn't done the green training, the divers were not beret qualified. Not that they minded. They were proud to wear their own blue navy beret. They were navy specialists who were masters of many trades. They had clocked up hundreds of hours in the water on all kinds of dive sets. They didn't run from bombs and mines, they took them apart. They could plant limpet mines on an enemy ship undetected. And now they were part Special Forces, elite assault troopers no less. They didn't wilt in the Regiment's cauldron of alpha-maledom – they thrived. And, ultimately, they emerged convinced that they were second to none in the Australian military.

In the CT squadron itself, there was absolutely no divide between soldier and sailor. They were teammates who had each other's backs and who built lifelong friendships. Going on line with CT squadron was the time of their lives.

The CT force consisted of two, sixty-man units, a land

troop and a water troop, with a dozen snipers seeded across both. The former was Alpha troop, comprised of SAS air operators – specialists in parachute and rope infiltration. The latter was Zulu troop, manned by 'water operators', both SAS and clearance divers. They could infiltrate from a submarine, surface craft or even helicopter. The men had pagers and would be on call twenty-four seven. They trained incessantly. They were never addressed by rank – first names or nicknames were used or else their call sign, a moniker that denoted troop, team and role within that team.

If your pager went off, you never knew if the call-out was for real. You said goodbye to your loved ones – again – and walked out the door not knowing where you were going or if you'd ever be coming home. More often than not the call-out was a validation shoot, a kind of spot check on your weapons proficiency. At the SAS range you'd be presented with a hostage scenario and told to storm a building. Standing outside the stronghold, you'd be shown photos of the terrorists and photos of the hostages. You were given an hour or so to get them clear in your head. Then you'd storm through the 'kill house', shooting the terrorists, sparing the hostages and heading straight out the back door for validation. Then it was, 'Okay, you can go home now.'

Scenarios were staged all over the country, and the CT squadron would fly in to conduct hostage-recovery exercises. They'd take down planes, buses, ships, 'embassies' – whatever stronghold had been prepared for them. Before a full-scale 747 mock-up was built for them at RAAF Base Pearce, forty kilometres north of Perth, they would descend on Perth airport under the cover of darkness to storm overnighting air-craft. Life was all fast-roping, parachuting, speeding cars and power boats, swooping choppers and open-sea diving. It was an action-packed existence lived at breakneck pace with the safety catch off. Occupational health and safety didn't exist. Nothing was a game. The explosive entry was live; the rounds were live; there were real people sitting in the room with the targets. And this was how they liked to impress their visitors.

'You used to have a guy standing in a room giving a talk to the VIPs – politicians – and either side of his head would be a figure eleven target – a man-sized silhouette target,' said Glenn Spilsted. 'When he says the words, "The one thing we've got on our side is surprise," the room goes black, charges are thrown in, the room's assaulted, lights come back on again – and the bloke's still standing there and there are two bullet holes in the targets on either side of his head. And the politicians are standing there thinking, *Geez, this is where our money's going.*'

The intensity was exhilarating, but spending a year in the CT squadron was just long enough to use up all nine lives. This was a thrilling highwire act with no net, and some paid the ultimate price. On 12 June 1996, a midair helicopter colli-sion during an exercise resulted in the loss of fifteen troopers from the Regiment and three members of the 5th Aviation Regiment.

'I remember flying sorties with the Blackhawk guys pre-accident,' remembered John Isles. 'We were doing some very scary things. Six or seven choppers in the air, three o'clock in the morning, three or four weeks into a rotor-blade exercise.

I was a sniper hanging outside on the sniper bar, looking down at the entry point that I had to cover for the boys to go in. I look down and there's the rotor blade of another helicopter below us, three metres from my feet. I pull myself up going, "Fuck!" And I can hear the pilots going, "Emergency! Sector blah blah blah!" And they go into their emergency procedure, whack the throttle to full stops. That pushes the helo below us down even further. We take off to the right and the pilot, as cool as a cucumber, goes, "Oh, we might try that one again without landing on a helicopter."'

Karl Price had a few moments that he thought would be his last. 'I've been in helicopters that have fallen sideways through the sky because they've flown over "the point" – from which you can't recover the craft – falling blade-first towards the ground,' he said. 'It's a daunting feeling when you're out on the skids of a chopper and you look between your legs and all you can see is sky.'

With a premium on shooting skill, the troops would live-fire three days a week, either on the move down an open range or storming the kill house. There was also the method-of-entry house – a stand-alone building that was shot at and blown to pieces then rebuilt, again and again. Then every six or seven weeks the water troop would head down to Bass Strait to dive in deep, cold water and big seas to carry out oil platform assaults.

Four teams of six men would swim in and run a line between two legs of the platform. The dive sets and fins, which fitted over boots, had karabiners to tie them off with. So the divers would stash their gear, surface and start climbing up caving ladders, armed with their swimmable weapons. Sometimes they didn't need a ladder: the bigger swells would lift them high enough to be able to grab onto the sea deck and jump over the guardrail. Usually, a pair of snipers went first. They would get themselves to an observation point to be the eyes of the troop in advance of the assault. Following their initial reconnaissance and reporting, they would provide covering fire as the rest of the troop climbed. They would move to the deck below the accommodation module, form up and launch the assault, sweeping through the entire platform. In time they knew the layout of every platform in Bass Strait and the North West Shelf intimately.

Dave Pearsall left the branch to become a commercial diver. The work led him back to the Bass Strait rigs but in a vastly different role. One day, looking up from the water at the overhead pipes snaking through the oil rig's decks, he remembered the covert 'free climbs' he used to do to infiltrate the platform. The divers would be in full gear, exiting the water after having swum for two kilometres at three o'clock in the morning.

'It was cold, slippery, there was shit hanging off everywhere. The adrenaline was pumping, and I'm trying to be as quiet as possible, trying not to slip, because if you did you would hit the pipes or decks thirty feet below,' said Pearsall. 'We had three decks to climb to the target, and only then did the important stuff start. Damn, it was fun, but God it was dumb. Back in those days we lived on the edge. Only our relentless training and can-do attitude stopped us from falling off.'

No matter how real the training seemed, the action was never for real. This heightened state of activity was essentially sustained in an artificial environment. They never got to put that training to operational use in the field. This was obviously a good thing for the Australian public, but an 'all theory, no practice' job was bound to have its downside. Some members found returning to normal clearance diving duties difficult. The comparatively slow life was a comedown. A few divers turned around and joined the SAS. For others, though, it was a relief to switch off from constant high-alert status.

Some divers who'd been on line at the Regiment did get the opportunity to work in a theatre of war, though as divers rather than counterterrorists. In January 1991, twenty years after the first incarnation was deactivated after Vietnam, Team 3 was stood up once more. Iraq had invaded Kuwait and Australia had joined the UN-sanctioned coalition to force Saddam Hussein's troops out. Completely out of the blue, the clearance divers were going back to war.

ELEVEN
NOTHING TO PROVE

GIVEN JUST FORTY-EIGHT-HOURS' notice, the twenty-three divers of Team 3 gathered at RAAF Base Pearce. Thirteen hailed from Perth and the remainder came from Sydney. As with Vietnam, those who weren't picked were gutted. 'Guys would have killed each other to get onto that deployment,' said Tim Hayes, who was among those overlooked. The team was liberally seeded with snipers and assaulters who had served in the SAS CT squadron. As a unit, the breadth of expertise was impressive. Four days after they assembled, they were in Bahrain, training and awaiting orders to move north.

It was early February 1991. Operation Desert Storm was two weeks old and still predominantly an air campaign. Maritime access to Kuwait remained blocked because of the

mine threat. The US-led coalition knew the Iraqi minelay-
ers had been busy in the Persian Gulf – in five months they
had laid around a thousand mines – they just didn't know
exactly where. An assortment of minesweepers, minehunt-
ers, Sikorsky choppers and EOD teams were out surveying
the waters. On 17 February, a mine countermeasures force
was threatened by Iraqi anti-ship missiles and had to move
out of range. After the threat had been neutralised, the force
went back to work. Just before dawn, one of the vessels, the
helicopter landing ship USS *Tripoli*, struck a contact mine.
The blast ripped a hole in the hull big enough to drive a truck
through. Three hours later, USS *Princeton*, a guided-missile
cruiser providing air defence for the group, detonated another
mine. The *Princeton* had slowed to a cautious crawl but had
unwittingly entered a minefield of Mantas – cutting-edge,
Italian-made, acoustic–magnetic mines that were shaped
like squat lampshades and lay on the sea bed.

Suddenly a Manta exploded under the *Princeton*'s stern,
shaking her violently for several seconds. The blast set off
another Manta 300 metres off her starboard bow. When the
second blast hit, a petty officer looking for mines over the
nose of the ship was pitched three metres into the air. Incredibly, the fire and flooding was contained and the *Princeton*,
severely buckled and torn, stayed afloat and on duty with
combat systems at the ready until she could be relieved.

The presence of Manta mines was of particular interest
to Team 3 members. They were expecting to conduct reconnaissance of Iraqi-held beaches in Kuwait and to survey and
clear them ahead of an amphibious assault by US Marines.

The divers would have relished the chance to sweep the shallows for mines and obstacles that might impede a landing force. However, not much was known about the Manta mine at the time. If any of the team came across an armed Manta, the magnetic signature of their diving set, although very low, may have been enough to detonate it. As it happened, the marines entered Kuwait overland from Saudi Arabia. While the ground war played out, Team 3 positioned itself at a staging post on the Saudi–Kuwait border and waited for the order to go in.

Four days after Kuwait was declared liberated and a ceasefire announced, the order to advance came. A convoy of three semitrailers and two trucks carried Team 3's twenty-five-tonnes of gear to the site of their first mission: a deepwater port forty kilometres south of Kuwait City called Ash Shu'aybah. The Iraqis had made a scorched-earth withdrawal. More than 700 oil fires were spewing from vandalised pipelines and wells. The facilities of Ash Shu'aybah were in ruins, but the coalition needed this port opened quickly so that the supply ships could unload and feed the ground troops. Team 3 and the American and British teams with them were given a week to make it safe.

Pockets of Iraqi resistance remained and the odd shot or blast could be heard as the divers went about their task. They were always heavily armed unless in the water. Part of the job was to clear the entire waterfront, so wharves, buildings and ships had to be searched for mines, booby-traps and ammo caches. The skills of the CT-qualified divers in the team were put to good use and, being expert weapon handlers, they were able to train up other team members who hadn't been through CT.

Chief Petty Officer Eugene Maxwell wrote in an account of the team's activities that clearing the port area meant 'crawling across a muddy seabed, with nil visibility, in a cold fourteen metres of water, using our hands as the primary sensors. [This was] nothing particularly new to us, however the possibility of a live mine or, worse still, a weighted corpse appearing out of the inky blackness was enough to send the heart thumping.'

The sun barely penetrated the black smoke of the oil fires. At times the team's work area had to be lit during the day. An untold quantity of oil was pouring into the sea. During every dive the men and their gear would become covered in sludge. Just keeping the equipment operational was a major task.

No mines were found in the port, but many contact mines had washed onto the surrounding beaches. While most of the divers were occupied with clearance dives, a small EOD team ventured out every day to neutralise the drifters. Getting to them was often the hardest part since the beaches were strewn with coiled razor wire. Also, the threat of land-mines meant the divers had to carefully prod their way towards each mine.

Come the week deadline, the port was alive with shipping. Team 3 was then assigned another port to clear, this time alone. Not long before, Ras Al Qulai'ah had been a functioning naval base – now it was a desolate wreck. Searching the waterfront buildings, the team discovered a mine factory. Here and there they came across failed Iraqi demolition charges, and scattered all over the place were unexploded cluster bomblets, plastic explosives, detonators and small arms. Thousands of pieces of ordnance were collected and destroyed. Once the waterfront clearance was complete, the diving began. The seabed was littered with a particularly lethal hazard left by US bombing raids – intact cluster bomblets. Hundreds of these hand-grenade-strength explosives were expelled over the target area with a carpet-bombing effect, but those that hit water failed to detonate. One careless kick with a fin could kill a diver and anyone near him. For this reason, the men kept a distance of twenty to forty metres between them.

The clearance of Ras Al Qulai'ah was completed in six days. From there, the team was sent to Kuwait City to rejoin the other coalition dive teams. The capital was fifty kilometres north of the oil fires, and so for the first time in three weeks the divers found themselves enjoying direct sunlight. Underwater visibility in Shuwaikh Port was no better than further south, though, and so once more hands served for eyes. The search was uneventful, even dull, but after being tasked to remove Iraqi corpses washed up and snagged on the beach wire, poring over the silty seabed was not so bad.

After almost two months, Team 3's work in Kuwait was done. In total, they racked up 231 dive hours, cleared 2,157,200 square metres of seabed, neutralised 234,986 pieces of ordnance, surveyed thirty-two wrecks, cleared seven ships and an untold number of waterfront buildings, and rendered sixty sea mines safe.

However brief, Team 3's Kuwait deployment clearly

demonstrated the clearance divers' operational worth under water. With advanced weapons skills they could also patrol and provide their own security while conducting EOD tasks. In short, Team 3 was an impressive, compact force package.

The whole dive branch took pride in Team 3's performance, even those miffed at being left behind. The Australians had searched and cleared more area than the British, Americans and Canadians combined. The British divers had dropped many of their war roles in the preceding years, focussing on deep diving and saturation diving, which may have been great for salvage work but not much use when it came to going into a conflict environment and clearing a port of malignant ordnance on short notice.

Following Kuwait, the British reprised their shallow-water mine countermeasure capabilities. The Americans established a new organisation to replicate the skill sets of the Australian clearance divers. To form their very own shallow-water EOD unit in 1992, they took recon marines who had back-of-beach capabilities, such as covert infiltration onto enemy land from water and the setting up of observation posts. They then took EOD divers who were experts in disposal and demolitions, and SEALs who had the weapons and tactical swimming skills.

'Our guys had the diving, demolitions and EOD all in one little packet and they [the US] didn't have that,' said Paul Darcey. 'The Americans and the Brits looked at what the Australian clearance divers had accomplished and they had to go back to the drawing board. Our blokes cleared four or five times the search area because they had the skill set in shallow-water environments – to be able to lay out a beach, do clearance.

'Kuwait was real kudos for us. It reinvigorated the way we did business. It proved to us that we are what we think we are – one of the best friggin' diving units in the world.'

≈

The Australian SAS played no part in the Gulf War, and the divers in the counterterrorism squadron liked to rub it in now and then, especially on Anzac Day. 'When you're good enough you'll get deployed, you blokes,' they joked. Over the years many lasting friendships were forged between divers and soldiers in the Regiment, so this was purely good-natured ribbing. You would have to be a very good mate to get away with having a dig at the SAS for not getting its nose bloodied in Kuwait. Unlike in recent years, the SAS back then was the Federal Government's force of last resort, and they were not particularly happy about it, especially seeing their British counterparts had gone behind enemy lines while they stayed home. Anyway, whatever humour value there was for the divers, they didn't get to enjoy it too long – by 1994, they were no longer part of the Regiment's counterterrorism strike force.

Despite the tight rapport that existed among the troops, the higher-ups decided to end the relationship. Some divers felt the Regiment was happy to let them go, or even squeeze them out. Karl Price saw the writing on the wall when he was basically told he had to serve under another trooper who was less qualified. To lead a team in the counterterrorism squadron you had to get perfect scores in all written and practical examinations. Price did so. As a team commander you had to control a multi-level, multi-room combat zone that took in elevators, lift wells and stairways. It would be a helicopter-in, live-explosive entry, live rounds flying. It was an extremely demanding, hands-on, mind-on role. But it was the position Price was qualified to do and expecting to take. One SAS warrant officer had other ideas.

'I was approached to take a subordinate position,' Price said. 'Some of their guys hadn't yet passed all the exams, but this warrant officer was trying to put me in a position subordinate to them. I said no. What I didn't know was that no one from navy would back me up.'

That Price ended up withdrawing over the matter marked the low point of his career. He had no choice. He packed his bags and returned to Sydney, the last petty officer in the Regiment.

By that stage, the split was already on the cards. It was fine for the SAS to provide a domestic counterterrorism capability, but there was no real field work to get stuck into. The CT landscape was changing. With the police forces having stood up their own CT squads, the SAS's role was getting marginalised, but perhaps they were just frustrated at being 'all dressed up with nowhere to serve'. So they changed the emphasis of their counterterrorism role, directing their focus on overseas recovery operations such as, say, rescuing Australian citizens, sporting teams or officials taken hostage, rather than trusting local militaries to do the job. To be capable of executing hostage recoveries on foreign soil, the CT squadron would need extra skills, such as high-altitude, low-opening (HALO) parachute insertions. For the divers, these add-ons would have meant an extra year in Perth.

'They [the SAS] sort of said, "If you want to stay on board, we need to get you for three years," which was untenable,' said Commander Peter Tedman. 'We couldn't sustain that capability as well as maintain all the clearance diving roles we had. So there was just a parting of ways. One year they came out of their capability conference and said, "We've re-roled ourselves this way, senior navy are unable to provide us with that support – see you later."'

In this light, Team 3's success in Kuwait was timely. The deployment had reaffirmed the branch's core identity: clearance diving. But to lose the CT role was a mixed blessing. For a decade, divers had been filing west to try out for the Regiment, and many younger divers were bitterly disappointed to miss out on the experience.

However, by 2002, the navy clearance divers were back in the counterterrorism business.

The SAS counterterrorism squadron based at Swanbourne was a five-hour flight away from the vast bulk of Australia's population, public institutions and target-likely assets. They were hardly a rapid-response option for the east coast. After Sydney won the 2000 Summer Olympic Games bid it was clear that a second special-response force was needed. Relocating the SAS east was not an option given the huge investment that had gone into their set-up. A new force had to be made from scratch.

The foundation was laid in 1996, when 4 RAR Commando was established at Holsworthy in Sydney's west. A number of SAS personnel transferred over to bolster the ranks of the new outfit. They were trained as a special strike force that could execute aggressive recovery operations on both land and sea targets. The whole tenor and scope of this new unit changed, though, in the wake of the 2001 attacks on the World Trade Center in New York. Preparedness for every kind of terrorist attack became an imperative. The Australian Defence Force revamped how its Special Operations Command would deal with chemical, biological, nuclear and explosive incidents. Part of that was a push to be cutting edge across all facets of counterterrorism. The Holsworthy commandos were named Tactical Assault Group East, code-named TAG East. A state-of-the-art training complex was built on the base, replete with indoor shooting ranges, fake town centre, mock jumbo jet and a 'shoot it down, build it back up' method-of-entry house. Of course, TAG East had to have a water capability, so the navy clearance divers were incorporated into the company.

The set-up was very different to the SAS operation. In this second-generation counterterrorism force, the divers formed one of three platoons, the other two filled by commandos. The divers operated under the army's Special Operations command, but day to day they were a self-run entity. There was no Cadre course this time, but to join TAG you had to pass an exacting Special Forces assessment: a four-week shooting and assaulting course. Once on line, just like their predecessors years before at Swanbourne, the TAG divers served as assaulters or snipers. And, again, they lived and breathed the use-it-or-lose training philosophy.

To keep their shooting honed they would be in the live-fire range three days a week, engaged in close-quarters battle training. A team moving through kill house scenarios – a layout of rooms, targets and corridors – was a rolling maul with weapons. A six-man team creates enough shooting and yelling to pass as an uprising. They have to shout because that is the only way to make themselves heard. If they are particularly well oiled, they snake fluidly in and out of room after room, covering each other, making sure there are no choke points, no bunch-ups, that nothing is offered around a blind corner, always shooting on the move. There's a kind of wolf-pack understanding, with roles interchanging as the hunt moves on, that can't be achieved by once-a-month practice. And what needs even more honing than the pack mentality is the vital skill of target discretion. At any time of the day or night there might come a call to gather and storm a stronghold, shoot the 'tangoes' (i.e. terrorists, from the phonetic alphabet T) while leaving the 'hotels' (hostages) unharmed. The whole point, after all, is hostage recovery. If they can't be cool-headed enough to take a microsecond to ID a target before pulling the trigger, they might as well just lob grenades into the rooms.

On top of their urban assault skills, the divers' platoon

gave TAG East its water capability. They covered all aspects of covert water operations, including diving, over-the-horizon insertions and water-borne assaults, which was of course a natural extension of their clearance diving expertise. But soon after TAG East was up and running, TAG-qualified divers were recruited for a job within Operation Slipper, the Australian Defence Force's counterterrorism campaign that encompassed the war in Afghanistan and naval patrols in the Gulf of Aden.

The Australians had kept a ship in the region since 2001, starting with an interception role against Iraq. In more recent years, the rising activity of Somali pirates demanded international intervention, so the Australian ships took on an anti-piracy role. This was not a role navy normally prepared for. The worst-case scenario in anti-piracy would be for a team to have to board a hostile vessel. Off the north coast of Australia, naval patrols might have illegal Indonesian fisherman trying to ram them or throw bricks as they climb aboard, taking care to avoid the spikes and barbed wire festooned over the vessel in honour of their arrival. Boarding a cargo ship overrun with pirates wielding AK-47s and RPGs is a different story. Generally speaking, this kind of small-fry hostility is not how the navy fights. The likes of a frigate punches with missiles and heavy-calibre guns at a distance. Ships do have their own boarding teams for maritime enforcement operations like trade sanctions, oil embargoes and people smuggling. But the expectation of violent, armed opposition changes the whole tone of the job and the skills required to handle it. For the anti-piracy role, a dedicated boarding party had to be accommodated on these patrols, and TAG-qualified clearance divers were the logical choice.

≈

A week after the Iraq War began in 2003, members of the reactivated Team 3 hit the water. The thirty-two-man team had been camped on the Kuwaiti border when the invasion started, and southbound Iraqi missiles landed close enough for the shockwaves to rock the divers in their tents. Eleven times in twenty-four hours they had to don gas masks and protective suits, responding whenever the alarm was raised for a chemical attack.

Given the order to roll, they headed straight for Umm Qasr, Iraq's only deepwater port. The first military confrontation of the war occurred here as British, American and Polish forces fought a fierce battle to win this prime strategic asset. Unlike the Iraqi Army and Republican Guards, the Fedayeen Saddam (Saddam's Men of Sacrifice) put up a stubborn defence of the port city. The battle lasted almost a week, with coalition tanks, heavy machine-guns, helicopter gunships and even Harrier jet air strikes all pitching in until the resistance was subdued. Once the port area was secured, there was an urgent need for it to be cleared.

Team 3 was joined by an American clearance team and a British dive unit. At this point all troops had become actors in what was at once a political, military and humanitarian emergency. US President George Bush and UK Prime Minister Tony Blair drove their nations, and others like Australia, into war with the primary goal being, as Blair declared, 'to disarm Iraq of weapons of mass destruction'. Amid the 'shock and awe' air and land invasion, Umm Qasr was perhaps the first indication that the war might not go so speedily as planned. In his eagerness to trumpet immediate success, US Defence Secretary Donald Rumsfeld declared that Umm Qasr had been taken and secured, which it would be – days later. Even then, pockets of resistance remained as Team 3 moved in. The imperative to clear the port stemmed from the need to show the invasion's human side. Before the war, more than half the Iraqi population was dependent on food aid, consuming 16,000 tons a day. The blockages enforced in the lead-up to the war resulted in a humanitarian crisis. Waiting off Umm Qasr was *Sir Galahad*, a Royal Navy supply ship holding 300 tons of food and water. Behind it were two Australian ships carrying 50,000 tons of grain each. On board *Sir Galahad* was a tribe of journalists. More were waiting in Kuwait to be bussed in under military protection to play their part in a politically choreographed event to show that, irrespective of WMD, bringing war to oppressed and starving Iraqis had a moving upside. On all fronts there seemed to be no more important job on the face of the earth than to get that Iraqi port open. Then there came some confounding news of a hold up – the Australian divers had found mines.

On their very first dive, working by feel alone, Team 3 divers located a sunken minelayer beside the wharf with four live mines on its trolleys. They were LUGM-145s, Iraqi-made contact mines, the same type that had punched a hole in USS *Tripoli* back in 1991. Given the desperate push to open the port, Team 3 immediately sought to free the mines and transport them to a safe area to be destroyed. With US SEALs and Australian divers maintaining security patrols, other members of Team 3 got on with the job of removing the mines to the tune of the odd exploding shell.

For mine countermeasures, the diving gear has to be acoustically and magnetically safe, so the divers were using their mixed-gas dive sets. The cylinders of these sets are made from a superalloy called Inconal, and they're spherical as opposed to cylindrical. Unlike the cylinder, the round shape doesn't form magnetic eddy currents as it moves through the water. The rest of the set is made of polycarbonates or rubber and other non-magnetic materials. The dive sets are rebreathers, which are acoustically safe – they don't make the gasping sound of a scuba regulator, nor do they expel noisy bubbles. Having mixed gas instead of pure oxygen gives the divers more time under water and reduces the time required to 'off gas', or breathe off the heightened levels of nitrogen in the blood. Donned in these state-of-the-art kits, the members of Team 3 had to approach the mines time and again by feel and, once disarmed, wrestle each out of its resting place so it could be lifted free and carried off to be destroyed. These were the only mines found under water at Umm Qasr, and when the Australians finally gave the all clear, *Sir Galahad* slid into the berth. The entire port was cleared in four days.

As the coalition forces advanced, they unearthed several weapons caches that Team 3 was called in to destroy. When a huge cache of forty-five LUGMs was found buried in the desert north of Umm Qasr, Team 3 destroyed them in clusters on the hour so that the massive blasts were not mistaken for enemy artillery fire.

The clearance work at Umm Qasr was entirely manual for the first few days. Then the divers were upstaged by the arrival of some specialist mammals. To much media fanfare, the Americans brought their dolphins in, as well as their UUVs (unmanned underwater vehicles) to help search the vast area of seabed. Both assets streamlined the divers' work. They would go in after the mammals or machines and reacquire and inspect only those items that were deemed suspicious, as opposed to all the other bits of rubbish that littered the seabed. The acute sensitivity of the dolphins' sonar meant they were able to detect objects that man-made sonar equipment – either handheld or fitted to the underwater vehicles – couldn't. Still, when the divers moved twenty kilometres north to clear another port, the dolphins did not join them because conditions were unsuitable. All the clearance work was left to the trusty divers.

When it came time to leave in early May, Team 3 had compiled a comprehensive work record that reflected their expertise and versatility. They cleared 2.5 million square metres of seabed and completed thirty-four EOD patrols, locating and clearing missiles (8), rockets (2), Mantas (6), LUGMs (35), limpets (4), RPGs (72), mortars (886), grenades (548), anti-tank mines (11), anti-personnel mines (4) and bombs (5), not to mention thousands upon thousands of projectiles, small arms and sundry ammo. It was an impressive haul. However the Iraq war may be remembered, or despite the reasoning of the US and UK architects of the invasion, Team 3 was sent to do an extremely difficult job in a conflict environment, and they exited having added another proud chapter to the war record of the branch.

Yet, in spite of the Iraq deployment and the divers' new role in TAG East, the branch was having difficulty holding on to divers. The money and opportunities being offered by private military contractors were simply too good to refuse for many divers, and the branch was struggling to replenish its losses. So when a soldier serving out at Holsworthy picked up the phone asking how he could go about becoming a clearance diver, he was made to feel particularly welcome. It was 2004 and the branch was hurting for numbers.

TWELVE
THE DE GELDER EFFECT

IF PAUL DE Gelder hadn't been so fed up with soldiering, he'd have tried out for the SAS instead of the navy's dive branch. But after five years with 3RAR, the parachute battalion based at Holsworthy, he'd had a gutful of the army. A six-month peacekeeping deployment to East Timor only made the infantry life back home all the more tedious. It was back to running around the bush looking for an invisible enemy, carrying a heavy pack, walking a long way and shooting guns and rockets. De Gelder was driven to do more with his life. If he wasn't progressing, he was stagnating. From the outset he was a soldier who looked onwards and upwards, wanting not so much to climb the ladder as to seek out the next challenge. At basic infantry training, de Gelder the shit-kicker would see the paratroopers walking tall in their maroon berets and think, *I want to be one of those guys.* Then once he was a paratrooper he would see SAS troopers wearing sandy berets replete with a 'Who Dares Wins' badge and think, *Fuck, I want to be one of* those *guys.* Then he was among a handful of paratroopers offered a three-month security gig in Iraq. It was only doing pickets – standing on a gate with a machine-gun – but it was operational, and that was the kind of rut-breaker de Gelder craved. But just as he thought life was about to get a little more interesting, the job offer was withdrawn. His motivation sagged. He was a dynamic, capable young man staring down a gun-barrel-straight career path – no surprises, no twists or turns, no mountain passes, just a few landmarks along the way denoting where he'd move up a rank. It was a vision he recoiled from.

'There was no way I wanted to be a forty-year-old soldier marching around the bush still, and I didn't want to be a crusty old warrant officer in the army, so I started to look for other options.'

A friend said he was going to try out for the clearance divers. When asked to explain himself, the guy lit up with enthusiasm. It was the kind of spark de Gelder knew he had lost. 'You know what?' he said. 'I want to be excited, too. I'll do it with you.' He was twenty-eight at the time and had never dived in his life. Three years later, he was a fully qualified clearance diver. And then he became the most famous clearance diver in the country. A chain of determined choices and hard-won achievements led him straight into the jaws of a bull shark.

≈

On the morning of 11 February 2009, de Gelder was part of a dive team called to Garden Island to help trial a new sonar detection system. Unlike most sonar gear, the new unit didn't have to be operated under water – it was supposed to be able to pick up a submerged swimmer from a ship's deck.

The divers came from Team 1, the sixty-man operational unit based at HMAS *Waterhen*. As with Team 4 in Perth, members here can elect to specialise in EOD and IED disposal. They are trained to tackle the kind of homemade bombs that were the main killers of foreign troops in Iraq and Afghanistan. As it happened, the two senior members in the five-man dive team that rode a Zodiac under the bridge and past the Opera House that overcast day were heading to Afghanistan in three months' time. Petty Officer Lane Patterson and Leading Seaman Jeremy Thomas, along with a third diver, were being assigned to the Townsville-based 1RAR, the next battle group rotating into Afghanistan. Unflappable and astute, Patterson was one of the most highly regarded divers in the branch. And even though he was only a few years younger than Patterson, de Gelder looked up to him as a diver to model himself on. Patterson was one of those guys that made you feel comfortable and safe whenever he was supervising. 'You're pretty blessed if you're working with Patto,' said de Gelder. 'No matter what's going on or how stressful, he'll always be able to keep a level head. He's the ideal diver.'

Once the dive team arrived at Garden Island, Patterson went ashore, boarded HMAS *Success* and positioned himself at the bow. It was around six o'clock. The city was rousing and the ferries were beginning another day spent criss-crossing the harbour. Patterson radioed Thomas, who had the boat positioned out near the small island of Fort Denison, and relayed the angle he wanted the first diver to approach the ship on. Thomas repositioned and put the first diver, Seaman Arthur McLachlin, into the water about 400 metres from *Success*. No dive sets were used: the initial test was to see how well the sonar device picked up a surface swimmer. After half an hour, Thomas told de Gelder to get in. You could say it was an order but not a barked command. In the divers' world, rank was respected but hardly imposed, and Thomas was de Gelder's rock-steady ally before he was his superior.

De Gelder loved the dive branch's relaxed but highly disciplined culture. Back in the army the first assembly of the day was a stiff, strict parade, all starched and polished, with a sergeant shouting orders into the still morning air. At the dive school, the seamen gathered, formed up, came to attention, went at ease and then listened to what the commanding officer had to say. He filled everyone in on the day's events, then they were dismissed to get into it.

Initially, de Gelder was shocked by the lack of regimentation. His very first taste of navy diving had been the ship's diver course. The supervisors handling the candidates were very strict, but they never shouted. All the guys taking the course struck him as competent, grounded individuals. They were all leaders – it wasn't like the navy had to try to turn them into such. During his initial testing, de Gelder was told he had the aptitude to take the officer path into the dive branch. He declined: 'I want to be out there getting dirty, not doing all the paperwork and planning. AB [able seaman] and kellick [leading seaman] are the two best jobs in the dive branch. I said I was happy being at the bottom of the ladder.'

Getting into the branch didn't just happen for de Gelder by firing off an email request. His transfer paperwork went nowhere for five weeks: a cooling-off period. He got frustrated time and again but kept tracking the progress and calling the dive school. Lieutenant Paul Darcey spoke with him several times. If Darcey knew there was potential in a young bloke, he gave him all the advice and encouragement he needed. And de Gelder had lots of potential. The selection course – CDAT – was murderous, but de Gelder loved it. He took strength from his determination to move his life forwards. 'Every morning, when I woke up on CDAT with my body aching, I'm going, *Why the fuck am I doing this?* Because I can't go back to the army!' De Gelder was one of the strongest in his course. Then came the real test – the formidable thirty-week basic-training course that turned you into a clearance diver, if you survived.

Four weeks before he was due to go on course, de Gelder suffered a hernia and was told he had to have surgery. He had the operation and then embarked on a gruelling nine months of training. 'It hurt so much. The only reason I got through the first couple of weeks was because I had such good people on course with me. They helped me out. I just did everything I could – put up with the pain and got through it. You really have to have that mental determination to get through that shit.' And of course de Gelder got through. He got his right arm rate – that coveted helmet patch. He'd done it. There was no looking back. Army was history, and it was on to Team 1.

≈

Once he reached the ship, de Gelder headed back to the Zodiac. He turned and began a second run at the ship. He'd gone just forty metres when he looked over his shoulder to check his line. Suddenly, something heavy slammed into his upper right thigh. No instant thought could make sense of it. He snapped his head back around and saw the broad head of a bull shark inches from his face. *Shark! A fucking shark!*

The shock of the absurd was overrun by a desperate order: *Go for the eye!* De Gelder tried, but his right arm wouldn't budge – his hand was caught in the shark's mouth. He tried with his left hand, reaching across his body. He had no leverage and his fist slid off the shark's nose weakly. The beast did respond to the blow, but not in the way de Gelder had hoped. Rather than relax its grip and let go, the shark bit down harder and shook de Gelder's body with frightening force, sawing its teeth through his flesh and bone. That's when the pain kicked in.

Thomas heard de Gelder yell out and looked towards his diver. There was nothing hysterical in de Gelder's cry, so initially Thomas assumed he'd cramped up. Then a burst of whitewater erupted and something large thrashed next to his mate. He saw de Gelder go under.

Thomas told McLachlin to get to de Gelder – fast. McLachlin wrenched the throttle. Thomas then radioed

Patterson: 'Patto! Shark!' He wasn't sure what was happening – he hadn't seen a fin – but he wasn't about to waste a second in case his worst fear was realised.

When he broke surface, de Gelder filled his lungs. He could see his own right fin sticking up in the air, and next to it the shark's tailfin. He was still pinned in its jaws. The shark took him under again, but when he surfaced the second time he knew immediately he was free to move. The shark had finally let go. *Free! Get the fuck out of the water!*

Turning to swim, de Gelder lifted his right arm out of the water. He saw a bloody, mangled stump where his hand should have been. *Fuck!* Just as he began to move, using side-stroke, the Zodiac appeared.

'As we got closer you could smell the metallic taste of blood,' said Thomas. 'It hit you in the back of the throat. I knew we had a severe haemorrhage. As we got closer we could see the plume of blood. The whitewater was red. I thought, *Fuck, this is serious. It's game on.*

'I made a conscious effort not to jump to any conclusion until I saw the injury. It could have been puncture wounds. Paul's body was in such a way that his leg didn't look connected. It looked like there were two parts of him. His groin area was submerged and you could see his fins pointing one way and body pointing the other.'

Thomas grabbed de Gelder's shoulders, McLachlin his legs, and Able Seaman Ryan Dart his waist. The three of them reefed de Gelder out of the water and onto the boat's pontoon, the thick, inflatable tubing that forms the Zodiac's sidewall. De Gelder could hear his mates swearing, and he realised there was something seriously wrong with his leg. The back of his thigh was gone – a horrific arc of a wound ran from his buttock to the back of his knee. A huge chunk of flesh had been removed, as though cut by machine. There was so much blood, yet the shark's teeth had missed the femoral artery by a mere centimetre. De Gelder fought against taking a look. For each and every diver in the boat now, victim and lifesaver, training manifested as instinctive action. De Gelder knew he might go into shock and die if he saw the gruesome horror of his injury. They laid him on the bottom of the boat. The relief of being out of the water was overwhelming; the sky above began to fade.

Thomas saw de Gelder's eyes roll backwards. He clenched his fist and punched de Gelder's chest repeatedly until he came to. He leant over and shouted. De Gelder roused, remembered his hand and looked at it again. *It needs a tourniquet.* He grabbed his forearm below what was now a stump, the shredded remains of his hand hanging by threads of skin. He kept his arm raised to stem the bleeding. Thomas stayed in his face, talking to him and demanding eye contact. *I have to stay awake. If I close my eyes I'm going to die.* The first-aid kit on the boat had no adequate dressing to deal with such a massive wound, so Dart and McLachlin took a lifejacket, jammed it into the back of de Gelder's leg and fixed and tightened the straps. McLachlin then sped the Zodiac towards the Garden Island wharf.

Petty Officer Patterson hadn't reached the wharf by the time the Zodiac arrived. He'd made calls, though. Police divers were on hand and an ambulance was en route. The waterline was three metres below the wharf, so a stretcher had to be fashioned to haul de Gelder up. When he finally arrived at St Vincent's hospital, he couldn't move, was struggling to breathe, barely had a pulse and was white as a sheet. De Gelder knew his hand was gone, but he offered the surgeon a case of beer if he saved his leg – he'd hate to lose it so soon after taking up surfing.

'When he came out of emergency,' said Patterson, 'he came past as I'm still shaking and washing his blood off my hands, and still trying to come to terms with it, and he's cracking jokes.'

The doctors were unable to save de Gelder's leg. They were hard pressed to save his *life*, and used 300 units (pints) of blood in the course of doing so. And there wouldn't have been any life left to save if not for the deeds of his mates out on the water. In the fifty-eight-year history of the dive branch, and in the hundred years since men in the Royal Navy's Australia Squadron had first dived to do hull repairs and salvage at Garden Island, not one navy diver had ever been attacked by a shark. De Gelder was at once the unluckiest diver and the luckiest man alive.

Early during his nine-week stay in hospital, de Gelder rid himself of self-pity. 'I taught myself not to have it. It's not going to help me achieve anything, so fuck it off. What's the point?' Lying there with a hand and an arm missing made him 'a bit upset'. He thought his life was finished, and at times wanted to end it himself. *What am I going to do now?* he wondered, but in no time that question became a driving force: *well, what are you going to do now?*

His answer was clear and unwavering: *I've got to get back*

to where I was before, and then better. Because what's the point of just being mediocre?

That's an extremely tall order: outdo other clearance divers with one hand and one leg? But no one in the branch would take offence or put limits on what de Gelder might achieve. In what seemed to be no time at all, he was walking freely on a prosthetic leg and shaking your mitt with a bionic hand. To get his career back on track he had to requalify in all the clearance diving skills. Within a year he was instructing would-be divers on gear assembly and maintenance; he was helping out on the scuba and deep-air courses and had joined the team that operates *Penguin*'s four-man compression chamber that is used to treat bends victims. That was all fine, but he was desperate to be back in the water, to be a diver again. He'd actually scuba dived just weeks after the attack. Six months later, he was in the water using oxygen rebreathers in the presence of navy medical assessors. To someone else, that would constitute miraculously rapid progress. For de Gelder it was painfully slow.

'I'm not even close to where I want to be,' he said. 'I have my own timeline and I'm way, way behind because of the bureaucratic structure. I can't be angry about it because I'd just be angry every day, so I have to be patient. At the same time, anyone else before this wouldn't have even got a look-in. They would have got a golden handshake, a beer and a "see you later". So I have to be thankful for that.'

For de Gelder the great thing about being a clearance diver was the full scope of all the skills mastered. He had loved every facet of his training. Explosives expert, scuba diver, covert diver, hard-hat diver, underwater metal worker: the diversity gave the job its richness. He saw every element as being vital – one part was nothing without the others – and he aimed to be nothing less than a fully qualified diver again.

Beyond all his requalifying hurdles looms de Gelder's ultimate goal: to be able to go on ops. That may well be mission impossible but, if nothing else, he needs that ambition to stay motivated and keep pushing though barriers. 'I'm not as light on my feet as I used to be,' he admitted in a rare nod to his limitations. But it's not just about whether he could do a job like, say, EOD – something that he would ultimately have to prove under rigorous assessment – it's also about whether he would be a good prospect to invest in. There are no passengers in this line of work – and no one, including de Gelder, has any illusions about that.

'I would love to be able to be deployed on exercises at least,' he said. 'I've done exercises in Malaysia and Singapore where I've done not much more than what I'm doing here at the dive school. I would love to get back to that point and have all the restrictions on my diving lifted.'

However far de Gelder goes to achieving this goal, few individuals in the branch's history could claim to have had a more profound effect on their peers and the dive branch as a whole. On the practical side, first-aid kits were bolstered and dive protocols changed to exclude the hours around dawn and dusk. Then there's what the young trainees see: a super-fit guy with half an arm and a prosthesis on his right leg jumping on and off boats, doing push-ups and heaves, and showing them all how it's done. He has them gob-smacked.

But de Gelder's most powerful effect might best be described as spiritual. Not in the sense of religious faith but in his own faith in the fighter creed. His affirmative optimism is damn-near all-conquering, defying you to stop him. To say he is a figure of inspiration is an understatement. He has lifted the spirit of every diver who ever passed through the branch. Undaunted, he is the striking reflection of their better selves. He remains governed by an unyielding fidelity to the warrior spirit, something he defines as 'the determination, even under the most intense pressure, to never give up'. These words are articulated by his deeds. He is very much alive but his spirit permeates the very woodwork of the branch like the revered fallen. As with surfers, all divers know the receded fear of being attacked by a shark. Divers live with that risk every day, and many have their own shark tales, but when they think of de Gelder they naturally question whether they could ever cope and respond in the remarkable way he has. Do they possess such depths of courage and character?

More than other divers, though, are some who ponder more solemnly the question of whether or not they could do a de Gelder: the IED operators bound for Afghanistan. A shark may have taken de Gelder's hand and leg, but amputations are the common injuries inflicted by high explosives. God forbid, these IED operators tell themselves, if I ever stuff up over there and lose an eye, a hand, a leg, a chunk of skull. God forbid I end up sobbing in a field hospital wishing life could be how it was but knowing it could never be the same again. God forbid I make a mistake that I would have to live with for the rest of my life, having to rely on loved ones to help me get by, maybe to even feed me, all because of one error of judgement. *I volunteered for this and now their lives must change radically to tend to my needs.*

In one terrible instant, you can be rendered unwhole. Escaping with your life is just the beginning. *If I don't come home in one piece, could I possibly hope to emulate de Gelder?*

Five months after the shark attack, Patterson and Thomas were in Afghanistan.

THIRTEEN
NO FISH OUT OF WATER

THE DAY AFTER Petty Officer Lane Patterson arrived at the Australian base in Tarin Kot, Uruzgan Province, Afghanistan, he was taken on a 'baby-sit' patrol by members of the departing battle group. Their beat, so to speak, was the Baluchi Valley, a few kilometres to the north of TK. Patterson was struck by the landscape's rugged beauty. Off in the distance the treeless expanses were fenced by jagged mountains. All around was desert, harsh and barren, save for the strips of verdant farmland that clung to the river. In amongst the lush fields and trees sat villages: mazes of mud-rendered walls, irrigation channels and residential compounds. Add donkeys, men with long beards wearing plain, flowing robes and it appeared to Patterson as if he had travelled back centuries. The military call these riverside corridors of civilisation the 'green zone'. Enchanted by the place, sleeping out under the stars at night and seeing Afghanistan with fresh eyes during the day, Patterson began to feel somewhat serene. The day after his first patrol, he was sent in to tackle his first bomb. That's when reality hit home.

'All of a sudden it was: "There's a bomb down there . . . It's meant to kill us . . . You're going to deal with it," ' Patterson recalled. 'It was a little surreal.'

For three years, Patterson had taught others how to dismantle bombs and mines. He was by any measure an expert in the EOD field. The way he had been trained to operate, the middle of an Afghan desert was fundamentally no different than being fathoms under the sea. The clearance diver learns to operate independently, working without direct supervision and making his own calls. Under water, you were on your own. Being down range over a bomb was the same. You worked in a small team, but that trio took complete responsibility for the task. Yet for all Patterson's EOD expertise he had no operational experience. Ten years earlier, he was a skinny grunge guitarist who had joined his father's cabinet-making business. He had a passion for scuba diving, but as far as earning potential went it was a dud career move unless you had the money for a commercial licence. He didn't. One day he just got jack of the drills and chisels. Covered in sawdust, he picked up the phone, rang the navy and asked if they had divers. He loved the life from the word go, worked his way through and posted to Team 1. He knew as soon as he arrived that there were opportunities to go to Afghanistan.

'I made sure I ticked all the boxes – fit, fast, ready to go,' he said. 'A little bit of self-promotion: "I want to go, boss. I'll do whatever you need." That's the way you have to work it. It's just like Civilian Street. I fell into it at the right time but definitely knew the job was on and pushed myself towards it.'

Patterson joined 1RAR for their lead-up theatre training. Before he could deploy, however, he had to be certified, which meant passing a comprehensive EOD assessment at the Australian Defence Force's Woomera facility in South Australia. Around forty IED personnel from army, air force and navy were assessed with him. If they passed, they were deemed to be safe operators and given the green light to go to Afghanistan. If they failed, they faced being left behind.

The men were tested over six days on various scenarios designed by Afghanistan veterans. The IED operators, or techs, had to pass three days in a row or they failed. It was a high-pressure environment. As a tech worked out how to deal with his roadside bomb using a robot, he would have examiners over his shoulder, pens in hand, ticking and flicking. He might not be as skilled as he should be at manoeuvring the robot and its manipulator arm. Using the remote controls, staring into the monitor, he has a few troubles. The digging tool doesn't expose any wire. The robot throws a track. The tech gets stressed and flustered; his judgement becomes clouded. He pulls on the bomb suit, walks down range and successfully dismantles the IED by hand. And that's a fail – he's taken the less safe option. Remote, remote, remote: that should be burned into his brain. In a tactical environment things might be different, but you won't get near a tactical environment if you don't pass as a safe operator. Patterson had a better grip on his emotions. When he found himself on the verge of getting flustered, he stopped, took a few deep breaths and made himself a coffee, slowing the whole process down. He was passed and sent back to Townsville.

Having clearance divers along for the ride struck most soldiers as plain weird. But if these snorkellers were keen to take care of their IEDs, then they were welcome. None of the soldiers were ever stand-offish or unfriendly towards the divers; they just hardly got to know them before they landed in Afghanistan. The odd warrant officer had issues, though. What was the world coming to when, in a land war, in a land-locked country, army jobs were being farmed out to navy? Few people outside the dive branch seemed to understand that the reason clearance divers existed at all was to counter the threat of enemy mines.

The shortfall in army EOD operators was nothing other than a reflection of how ubiquitous the IED had become, at first in Iraq and then Afghanistan. Commander Steve Bliss was a clearance diver who was sent to Iraq to share his EOD expertise. He ended up leading Task Force Troy, the coalition's counter-IED unit, to deal with the proliferation of the insurgents' deadliest weapon. Bliss saw how the Australian army couldn't cope with the sheer scale of the IED threat, and he pushed for the navy to get divers in to help out. 'I could see the hurt army was in, and we weren't providing suitable coverage to our troops on the ground,' he said. 'Army didn't have the numbers to be able to provide EOD support.'

Like many an army officer, navy brass believed a land battle was exclusively army territory, and many senior officers didn't understand what clearance divers actually did. Bliss persisted. Other divers followed in his footsteps, aiding the US army's effort to keep up with the rapid pace with which IED technology was evolving. From the simple victim-operated bomb to massive bombs to roadside daisy chains to shaped charges that could pierce the body of a Hummer with ease, the world of the IED was getting more and more sophisticated. Afghanistan had trended the same as Iraq – IEDs rapidly went from nuisance value to number-one killer, and a smart killer at that. Bliss's efforts finally paid off, but not in Iraq. Divers, along with air force EOD operators, began to be incorporated into the Australian ground forces in Afghanistan.

≈

It was coming up to sunset when Patterson and an air force tech were dropped off a few minutes' walk from the IED. The vehicles, and the 130-kilogram robot they carried, could go no further. They pulled back to provide cover with their heavy guns. Soldiers led them to the IED, which had originally been spotted by a member of the Afghan National Army unit the Australians were mentoring. Three mortars had been taped together and positioned on the roof of a walled compound. A grenade fuse was lodged into the mortars, and a length of kite string was attached to the fuse. The rig was set up for an insurgent to watch and wait for a passing patrol, pull the string, function the fuse and explode the mortars at head height. How many patrol members would have been killed deepened solely on the distance they kept between themselves.

This was no training run. An army patrol was now looking at Patterson like he was the boss, asking him what he wanted them to do. A heavy sense of responsibility weighed upon him. The diggers had set up a cordon eighty metres around, the nearer men finding a wall or tree for cover. The cordon was far closer than would be allowed in training, but the integrity of the patrol had to be maintained. Keeping the unit intact was paramount. The Taliban would definitely be watching. Any lack of cohesion could be an ambush opportunity. An army tech from the outgoing battle group was on hand to help manage the job. The soldiers had to maintain a clear zone all around the bomb, keeping locals back with orders in Pashto they were still struggling to get their heads and tongues around. Once the cordon was set, Patterson went and had a look.

The robot was not an option and neither was the bomb suit. Weighing around sixty kilograms, the suit was also portable only by vehicle. Deep in the network of narrow tracks that interlaced the green zone, you had to make do without. Not having the two main safety items wiped out much of the procedures so diligently learned and then scrutinised at Woomera. Patterson ended up doing something that would never be taught or passed at home: he disconnected the IED with his knife. Half an hour later, he walked away with the components in his backpack.

Patterson went back to the site to make sure there were no secondary devices. Inside the compound, he found a barn adjacent to where the IED was found. As he began to probe some loose dirt he suddenly heard footsteps behind him. With the cordon in place, no one should have been there. Patterson dived to the ground and drew his pistol. He found himself looking down the barrel gun at a little girl. She was staring at him, as though asking, *What on earth are you doing in our barn?*

≈

Thomas arrived a few weeks after Patterson and, along with another diver, Petty Officer Mick Oaklands, they formed an all-divers EOD team. Oaklands was a tech like Patterson. Thomas did reconnaissance, which meant that in various ways he had their backs. He was trained in IED disposal but not quite to operational level, so he prepared the tools for the techs, kept watch while they got on with the job and gave his two cents' worth when they put their heads together. This team was busy the whole nine months of the tour. IEDs accounted for more than half of foreign troop fatalities in Afghanistan. That's not to say the Australians hadn't been engaged in fierce combat, but the prevalence of IEDs meant they patrolled and fought in a minefield. A few months before Patterson arrived in country Sergeant Brett Till, an army tech, had been killed attempting to disarm an IED. He was Australia's tenth fatality. Patterson had only been in the country a couple of weeks when he witnessed an IED blast that killed Private Benjamin Ranaudo and took Private Paul Warren's leg.

It was a steep and dire learning curve but Patterson got accustomed to the job quickly, and he absolutely loved it. The initial feeling of being overwhelmed and not in control of that first scenario evaporated with his first success.

The Australians spent the bulk of their time in patrol bases. These were platoon-sized camps enclosed by blast walls that served as forward-operating bases. They got a few days a month back at TK, but other than that the platoon base was home. Late in the tour they would occupy the odd abandoned housing compound they'd found.

'We would move in as a platoon and occupied it, sometimes for months,' Patterson said. 'We'd interact with the locals and be right down amongst them in the middle of the night. That really caused some dramas for the Taliban as far as them being free to operate and manoeuvre. That was the highlight for me: living amongst the locals. You're in the fight every day and night down there.'

The initial patrols of the tour, though, were motorised where they'd travel in or walk alongside their Bushmaster armoured vehicles. Mutual respect and friendship was established quickly between the soldiers and divers. There was a strong feeling on patrol that they were a complete and highly capable unit.

'I felt safe,' said Thomas. 'If we got into a scrap we had the firepower, skill and professionalism to deal with it. Of course there's going to be a stray round, but you can't dwell on it too much. That's just the nature of the business. But if the searchers could find it, we could deal with it. And if we got into a fight, the infantry could deal with it.'

The searchers were human minesweepers, young engineers who led the way with their metal detectors and dogs. These sappers had the most dangerous job in Afghanistan by far: they walked into the unknown with every step, sweeping their detectors constantly. Typically aged under twenty, they led the patrols, taking full weight of duty and responsibility for the lives of the men that followed. Nagged by the terrible prospect of an IED going undetected, they kept a trained ear tuned to the warped, high-pitched squeal coming through their headphones. At the same time, they would cast an educated eye over the landscape ahead. They looked for any sign of a bomb – like, say, a wire dangling in a tree that could be a receiver for a remote control detonation – and they looked for likely places to bury a bomb or a weapons cache.

Scouts followed behind the searchers, then came the bulk of the patrol, and then the EOD specialists as the tail-end Charlies. The divers weren't assigned to every patrol, but when they didn't go out an IED would invariably be found and they would have to go out anyway. When the searchers located a bomb – and even when the patrol took enemy fire – it was a relief because at least you knew what was going on. At all other times, everything was unknown.

How the locals received the Australians varied from one village to the next. Even in the same village the mood could change in a hundred metres. One minute they would be feeling at ease with the locals, people smiling at them, patting them on the back and offering food. Turn the next corner and the reception might be stone cold with no one wanting to be seen anywhere near them. A patrol of twelve kilometres might take them through two or three Taliban-controlled areas alternating with friendly ones. Sometimes the difference would happen overnight after the Taliban had moved through. They could come in and post letters that contained dire warnings against those who cooperated with foreigners. They might hang a tribal leader who had dealt with the Australians, and weeks or months of hard-earned trust and understanding would be obliterated. A village that had been friendly and hospitable the day before was now frosty and silent. This type of vibe was also a fair indication there was an IED in the vicinity.

In the unfriendly areas, patrol members knew they were rubbing shoulders with the enemy. After a patrol passed through most villagers resumed going about their business. Others just stood and watched the patrol go.

'When you caught their eyes, you knew,' said Thomas. 'They'd had some form of military training. The faces and eyes of the insurgents said it all.'

The Australians had to get used to the fact that their every move was being watched. Patterns of movement and rest were kept varied: being predictable made it easy for the Taliban to decide where to bury an IED. There was a weird and discomforting intimacy to this battle, and for EOD operators like Patterson the job just got more and more personal. At the beginning of his tour the Taliban were indiscriminately targeting vehicles and foreign personnel with their IEDs. By the end, Patterson was on a hit list. The Taliban got so fed up with having their bombs discovered and dismantled that they began setting traps to lure and kill IED operators.

≈

The Baluchi Valley was part of a long infiltration route feeding Taliban weapons, fighters, bombers and know-how from Pakistan into Helmand Province. This insurgent trail ran from the Afghan border province of Zabul westward into Uruzgan and then south to where the fighting was heaviest. A key aim of the Australian forces was to disrupt this flow. The retaliation directed at them often revealed a lot about how the tactics of Taliban bombers were evolving. Uruzgan was upstream on this feeder route, so new Taliban techniques were often employed here before Helmand. One of Patterson's finds had repercussions across the entire theatre: an IED that was virtually undetectable by metal detector.

One day searchers clearing a road in advance of a vehicle convoy reached a dry-river crossing and hit on a metal contact. After a little probing they found a battery pack and some wires. The battery pack was typical – a bunch of D cells stuffed end on end into a tyre tube. Individually, the D cells produce 1.5 volts. A pack like this could generate over 20 volts – ample to fire a detonator. A means of sending that current into a detonator must have been nearby. With roadside bombs, this would typically be a pressure plate switch that fires the bomb when a vehicle runs over it. But the sappers picked up nothing else with their detectors. They moved out, called EOD and Patterson arrived with Thomas and Oaklands.

Oaklands steered the robot down range, dug up some wires and before long unearthed a pressure plate. Like most pressure plates, it was made from two planks of wood nailed together but kept apart by small blocks at both ends. Even when buried, the weight of a vehicle will push the top plank onto the bottom one. Usually, the inner side of each is lined with a metal strip wired to a battery and a detonator. When the two pieces of metal touch, the circuit is closed, the detonator fires and a large container filled with fertiliser-based explosive becomes a blast powerful enough to flip a ten-ton armoured vehicle and inflict untold impact damage upon the occupants. What was unusual about the pressure plate Oaklands pulled out was that it was vitually non-magnetic. Instead of lining the planks with metal, this bomber had used carbon rods taken from the cores of household batteries. They conduct electricity but are non-metallic, so there was hardly a magnetic signature for the sappers to pick up on. After ripping the wires free using the robot, Oaklands walked down in the bomb suit to look for the main charge. He found a palm oil container filled with twenty kilograms of explosive. He put a counter charge on it, took cover and blew it up.

The searchers moved back in and about twenty metres further along they hit another metal contact, smaller than the first. It was another battery pack, this time made out of a stack of coin-sized watch batteries. It seemed this IED was targeting any vehicle responding to the first IED. The wires broke when Patterson removed the battery pack, so he was uncertain where they led. He scaled a nearby spur to look down on the site with his binoculars, trying to figure out how the IED firing system and charge would be laid out. It was then he noticed a camp of Pashtun nomads, known as *kuchis*, nearby – or rather he noticed someone in the camp who was definitely not a *kuchi*. Among the group was a particularly well-groomed man. He was being looked after, served tea. Patterson walked towards the camp armed only with a pistol, but he kept it holstered. The man's clothes were spotless, and his long tunic was cut square at the bottom, a style favoured by Pakistani tailors. When he saw Patterson, coming he rose quickly, left the *kuchis* and headed straight for the green zone.

'He'd been hiding in the *kuchi* camp, watching us the whole time, and no one had picked up on it,' said Patterson. 'I was in no way equipped to run him down, but it was obvious – the Taliban had been watching us conduct that task from only eighty metres away.'

Patterson turned his attention back to the second IED. They spent an hour or so working remotely, using the robot to dig into the dirt and gravel in the hope of finding the pressure plate and a lead to the main charge. They were getting nowhere, so Patterson walked down range for an initial 'clean skin' visual inspection, leaving the bomb suit behind. No vehicles could use the road until it was completely cleared. When Patterson returned, the two operators agreed that they had to park the robot and go dig for the bomb by hand wearing the bomb suit.

Besides providing protection against flak, the main safety element of the bomb suit is its weight. At sixty kilograms, it will stop you – up to a point, of course – from being picked up and hurled through the air by a blast wave. It also helps keep your limbs and head attached to your torso. Reassuring as that may be, the bomb suit is not the most ideal workwear, particularly if you're standing under the midday, midsummer Afghan sun. Patterson and Oaklands took half-hour turns in the suit, walking down range and excavating the bomb area, employing all the patience of an archaeological dig. The ambient temperature soared into the forties, and to God-knows-what inside the suit. Their visibility was hampered by visor fog and their manual dexterity compromised by the thick gloves. Persevering, they eventually unearthed the pressure plate. All that remained was the main charge, which might be booby-trapped. Eventually they decided to ditch the suit and excavate the site slowly and methodically by hand in a grid pattern. If they stuffed up, they were dead. End of story.

'That decision to me was confronting,' said Thomas. 'At that point, it was, "Okay, job on. Straight to the point." But you could see in their faces the realisation that this is what they had to do. They'd exhausted all other means.'

Patterson and Oaklands took it in turns to lie down and dig into the dirt road with a small trenching tool to a depth of a foot. They tag-teamed until the sun went down. Finally, by torchlight, they found the main charge and detonated it.

Like the first pressure plate, the second also featured carbon rods. Intel had been reporting that the Taliban were using them to avoid their switches being detected – they also used copper speaker wire for the same reason – but no one had yet retrieved a sample. This find had significance for all coalition troops throughout the Afghan theatre, particularly the searchers. Their job had become that much more dangerous.

Patterson immersed himself in his work. Every aspect fascinated him. The research, the reports, what other techs said and thought – all of it allowed him to build a detailed picture, an enhanced situational awareness, of what was going on in his area. It was a very fluid environment: what an EOD operator encountered in Helmand or Paktia or Kandahar today might crop up in Uruzgan tomorrow. As for the Baluchi Valley, such things as the degree of hostility, the number and size of weapons caches found and the level of IED activity revealed how Taliban tactics were trending in the short-term. For Patterson, no detail was too small or insignificant – it might inform a future decision that his life depended on. But research was one thing – after spending too long stuck inside the base, Patterson and Thomas would be stinging for a call-out.

'You're hanging out for the next job,' said Patterson. 'You really want it to happen. You start to go a little bit loopy; there's no doubt whatsoever. You're waiting around, bored, and as soon as you hear on the radio that someone's found an IED somewhere, that's it – the adrenal gland dumps all that adrenalin and we'd be standing with our packs on and our rifles twenty minutes before anyone else, ready to move. It's very addictive, very exciting.'

The Australians picked up insurgent chatter on their comms. Translators, or 'terps', would relay the conversations.

'The bomb guys are here,' a voice would say when the EOD team arrived. Knowing that the Taliban was watching you work on their IEDs was disconcerting. Of course, the infantry cordon was ordered to confiscate phones and to even shoot anyone suspected of trying to detonate the bomb using their phone, but even when there appeared to be no observers in the vicinity, they would still hear Taliban commentary of their actions. Ultimately, you had to accept that the enemy was your audience. And the best countermeasure for that was to be unpredictable. It was tempting to follow the same course of action with the more standard disposals. Once the battery pack and switch were disconnected, you would uncover the main charge, put a countercharge on it, walk away and detonate. Do that too many times, though, and you'll walk into a booby-trap. Patterson rarely took the most direct, logical approach to an IED. If the bomb was in a hallway, he wouldn't enter the house via the front door. Chances are there would be trip-wires or pressure plates set. Instead, he'd climb in through a back window. The Taliban observers watching Patterson dart here and there, taking any entrance into a building bar the front door, referred to him as the 'energetic one'.

Thomas, who originally hails from Papua New Guinea, was 'the dark one'. If Patterson was down range he might hear Thomas's voice through his earpiece: 'Patto, they're watching. They've just reported you walking towards the device.' And when the team dismantled another one of their IEDs, the Taliban no doubt called them every name under the sun. The IEDs may have been assembled from what we consider scraps – speaker wire, auto parts, bolts and nails as frag, fertiliser – but each bomb was a considerable investment of the Taliban's time and money. Instead of enjoying the glory of killing infidels, they were left nursing the bitterness of defeat, which turned their minds to removing the thorn in their side.

The bomb disposal business has always been personal to some degree. It's always been a one-on-one battle. Sometimes the fight is uneven, such as when a low-level Taliban operative lays a very simple IED that is easy to detect and dismantle. Bombs like those are easy pickings. Well-trained operatives are a very different story.

'Some date as far back as the war with the Russians, when they were part of the mujahedin,' said Patterson. 'They have real cunning and guile, and are very hard to catch. They operate like a drug dealer would in Australia: they don't do or handle anything themselves; they just offer info, advice and direction.'

Taliban bomb-making handiwork can be quite sophisticated and difficult to defeat. If they can't find electric detonators, they can use the non-electric variety. Normally these would be fired by contact with a burning fuse, but the Taliban will take tiny Christmas lights, break off the glass bulbs and place the filament in contact with the detonator. Instead of lighting up a Christmas tree, it triggers an IED blast. Everyday remote-control technology is used. The key fob car-locking system, for instance, can be rigged into a switch. Phones, of course, can too. When you can hear Taliban chatter discussing what you are doing near their bomb, when you have no idea where they are watching from, so your snipers can't pick them off, and when you suspect the device is rigged to fire by remote control and they are just waiting for you to get close enough before making the firing call – that's a pretty tight day at the office.

'That's one of the worst things you come up against, mainly because you don't know whether you have control of the situation,' said Patterson. 'If something's victim operated, like a pressure plate, you basically have control of the situation. Whether you live or die is up to your actions down range. With remote control, you don't have that surety.'

As the weeks passed, Patterson got to know a few bombers. The way the IED was configured, the way the wires were twisted, the way the battery pack was made – all could be fingerprints identifying the same hand. *Ah, it's you again.* Some of the most creative and dangerous devices betrayed the bomber's identity; Patterson would know for certain that he was dealing directly with a trained operative. Putting the bomber's logic in reverse was akin to reading his mind: he could see how much effort, thought and planning had been invested in the trap; how the bomber had tried to outwit the infidels, conceal his device, inflict the deadliest toll possible.

Patterson might even know the bomber's name through various bits of intel. He could tell where he had trained – Pakistan, Iran, even Chechnya. He knew it wasn't some local farmboy following handwritten instructions; the guy knew he had to innovate to stay effective, and he had the skill to do so. He would try new things, alter his tactics. He'd target vehicles one week, dismounted patrols the next. Instead of using the usual palm oil container to carry the charge, he might opt for pressure cookers with nails added. He might lay multiple devices and plan ways to catch someone like Patterson, to lead him to his death. A bomber like this was a game-changer.

It was when Patterson arrived in the country that the Taliban in the Baluchi Valley turned on IED operators. This new development was discovered accidently by a Dutchman. He had found what he thought was a simple IED. He pulled it apart, traced the wire to the main charge and started to dig. Upon lifting a rock, he saw something that must have turned his blood cold: a nail sticking up through the soil. He would have known that the nail was part of a homemade pressure-release switch. It was supposed to spring up when the rock was removed. That would bring two metal contacts together and blow the IED. As it happened, grains of dirt had jammed the nail so it wouldn't rise. The Dutchman was standing on top of a twenty-five-kilogram bomb – exactly where the bomber wanted him to be – and was alive by sheer luck. He was very quiet for days afterwards.

This find changed everything. IEDs were now being used as lures to draw operators into other IEDs. By the end of Patterson's tour, the Taliban were targeting operators and searchers almost exclusively.

'One thing the Taliban have got is that there's only one person in the Australian forces that they can bring to a certain mark on the ground, and that's the EOD operator,' said Patterson. 'All they've got to do is bury a wire and they know we have to come and deal with it. You do feel vulnerable, but every bomb you pull out of the ground, especially these pressure-releases and stuff that they were targeting us with, is a great victory. It's a boxing match.'

The Australians started to find more and more booby-trapped jobs. Sometimes the Taliban would plant an obvious IED, knowing the locals would see it and tell the Australians. And, sure enough, once inspected the Australians would discover that the IED was fitted with some sort of anti-lift or anti-handling device. On one occasion a courageous boy stopped an Australian patrol and told them he knew where an IED was buried. He led them to an intersection and, without pointing, informed the patrol that an IED was buried a metre to the left of his foot. He then walked away. Unwittingly, the boy had done exactly what the Taliban had wanted him to do.

The two sappers who first searched the area found nothing. A week later, another local insisted that there was an IED buried in the same location and that they had to take a good look. They did so and again found nothing. Patterson had dealt with a booby-trapped IED nearby on the same stretch of road – a remote-control job – and he was told the same man had buried this latest one. Patterson probed around here and there to no avail. The next day another patrol noticed a fresh groove had been cut into the road. There was a wire protruding from it. Patterson and Warrant Officer Jeramie Faint, an army operator, returned to the site, certain that the wire had been placed there to draw them back in. Faint traced the wire, but it wasn't connected to anything. After digging around a little, he exposed an anti-removal device. Again, it was a nail switch with a rock placed on top of it. Luckily, the soldier hadn't disturbed the rock.

'I had a very sick feeling about this job,' said Patterson, who was watching Faint from eighty metres away. 'I saw him do a little head bob as he took a second look at what he was uncovering, then he got up and skipped away. He took a walk about twenty metres away to calm himself down.'

For over a week the Taliban had been drawing the Australians in, manipulating them in the hope that an operator would finally take the bait and lift that rock. Fortunately, they failed. The mine was countercharged and the area cleared. There was added satisfaction in getting rid of a device like that: they had foiled an assassination plot against themselves.

The lethal grudge match nature of IED warfare is partly why Patterson found the job so utterly addictive. From getting called out to walking alone down range, the entire experience was a rush. Half the joy of winning was the savouring of the enemy's defeat.

Patterson knew this feeling well but never more so than when he dismantled a huge pipe bomb he found buried in the road. He had spent hours tackling the device – stalking it, really – working his way in from all angles before eventually unearthing a six-foot long metal pipe. The bombmaker had taken a section of bore casing used for drilling wells and stuffed it with explosive and ball bearings. On detonation the case-hardened steel would have shattered into long, razor-sharp shards. If a foot patrol had set the device off, there would have been multiple deaths and amputations. This was certainly a unique IED that had taken a lot of work to create.

When Patterson finally pulled the forty-five-kilogram pipe bomb out of the ground, he took it in both hands and lifted it above his head. He turned full circle triumphantly to show the enemy, wherever he was, the corpse of their assassin.

Once the device was countercharged, Patterson took a break. A few Afghans began gathering around the site and a tall, well-dressed man walked down to join them. He had an air of authority about him, yet he was clearly not a local. He did not mingle with the Australians, or the villagers for that matter. He cast his eyes over the ground where the bomb had been buried, and it seemed to Patterson as though he was trying to work out how on earth his grand plan had come to nought. If this wasn't the Taliban bomber himself, he was definitely the man they paid to lay it. Finally, his gaze locked on Patterson.

'I was lying in a paddock, covered in sweat, eating,' said Patterson. 'He looked straight at me. He'd been watching me do his bomb and destroy it, and the look of utter hatred he gave me was unbelievable.'

In reply, Patterson smiled and stuck his finger up at his rival. The man glared back and stormed off.

The longer Patterson spent in theatre the more personal the job got. After a while the bounds of perspective got blurry.

'After doing job after job after job, you start to go a little bit loopy,' Patterson said. 'It's a high to have done a job that's dangerous like that, like you could never experience any-where else. That may not be a healthy attitude, but it's one that develops towards the end of the trip, so it's probably a good idea to get out of there before you take it too far.'

And for all his accumulated skill, experience and awareness, the thing that kept Patterson alive was that most fickle of allies: luck. During his tour he had seen men live and die by the most inexplicable whims of chance.

'Every job has five per cent of luck in it,' he said. 'So at one stage or another you're going to run out of lives. No matter how good you are, the Taliban are going to trip you up or something's going to go wrong. And it could be as random as they've made an IED very poorly and, just by the wind blowing or an animal moving past, two wires touch together and it explodes when you're down there. It can be that unlucky.'

Fortunately for Patterson, Thomas and Oaklands, their luck held out for the duration of their nine-month tour. They returned home to mentor those following in their footsteps.

FOURTEEN
FOLLOW ME, BOYS

'WAR IS WHAT all this is about,' said Lieutenant Paul Darcey. By 'this' he means a variety of things: the diving school where he currently works, the good-to-go Teams 1 and 4 at HMAS *Waterhen* and *Stirling*, the clearance divers posted onto mine-hunters, the divers out at TAG East, the underwater repair divers. The rigorous cycle flows from selection training to more training to exercises and again back to training. And every once in a while comes the acid test every diver quietly craves: the tactical operation. 'People who aren't in our profession might look at that and go, "What do you mean you want to go to war?" They just don't understand.'

Perhaps it is more difficult to embrace than understand. A military career that ends with no operational mileage on the clock may be full, rewarding and distinguished, but it will not be complete. The dive branch has been preparing men to be war-ready for sixty years. Divers have been engaged in active duty for less than five years of that time, with only a minority taking part in hostilities. The scarcity of this front-line experience only enhances its perceived value.

Darcey knows this more than most. Throughout his entire career as a clearance diver – thirty-five years and counting – he has amassed a grand total of six months' operational experience. He was sent to Iraq in 2008 to join Task Force Troy and help thwart the use of a particular type of IED that had rapidly become an extremely serious threat: the EFP, or explosively formed projectile. Triggered by the kind of laser sensors that detect home intruders, these bombs fired a large molten-copper bullet at a mile a second into the victim, which was usually a vehicle. Even armour a half-foot thick didn't provide sufficient protection. Not only were EFPs proliferating, but the firing systems were getting smarter. The toll on American vehicles and their occupants was shocking. The US devoted a mind-boggling amount of resources to tracking down the perpetrators and component suppliers, and devising ways to counter the enemy's tactics. Darcey had the highest US security clearance for the role – he would be in meetings with generals where colonels had to leave the room. But while the rotation was a mere fragment of his life's experience, it was potent and rewarding, and it was what he needed to fulfil his professional career.

On most days, though, Darcey will cheekily dismiss wartime operations as being 'all that Gucci stuff', as though deployments are fancy-pants parades in which you get to wear all the gear and wield all the gizmos. The glint in his eye makes it clear there is no disrespect intended; it's more a reminder that here, around the dive school at *Penguin*, and over at *Waterhen* and *Stirling* and Holsworthy, is where the bulk of the branch's work gets done, day after day, year after year, in peace. The branch has been Darcey's chosen life; he would be a bitter man if he had spent it just waiting to go to war. He first walked through those gates at the top of *Penguin* in 1976, in search of a career. Instead, he found a calling.

Back then the Vietnam stories were still fresh and exciting, but the Vietnam War itself was well over. In the 80s he tried out for the SAS counterterrorism squadron but was failed. The rest of that decade passed with divers doing little else but training, unless you were over with the SAS. There were channel clearances and EOD work carried out in the Solomon Islands and around the Pacific – good, hands-on diving and demolitions – but no operational jobs. A lot of guys left to be commercial divers. Darcey didn't want to leave.

When the Gulf War came along, he was working right where he is now, manning the course implementation officer's desk. He was a warrant officer then, one of the most senior and experienced clearance divers in the branch, but he was in the wrong place. The diving school is where you spend your days instructing, unlike Teams 1 and 4 where you are kept in a cycle of operational readiness. If he had posted into either team at the time, he would have been off to Kuwait. The memory of missing out is still barbed.

'There was a lot of envy – not that it was voiced – among the senior guys like myself at the time. I thought, *Geez, here*

I am.' He grimaced good-naturedly as he said this. Then he sighed and let the thought go. 'Ah, well. Shit happens.'

Not everyone wants to spend their entire careers as a navy diver, but there have been times when the exit rate has been a concern. The Iraq war brought this issue to a head. In 2004, eight senior clearance divers left the branch in one hit to go and work with American contractors in Iraq, doing the specialist EOD work they were trained for – and for five grand tax-free a month. This exodus was a major drain, and the branch took years to recover those ranks. But now there were clearance divers in Afghanistan making a hell of a difference. They had destroyed at least 200 Taliban IEDs in Afghanistan and suffered only one minor injury. Every diver back home took pride in that – the ripple effect of deployment.

Year after year, the diving school provides a service to the teams. Novices walk in and qualified clearance divers walk out, competent in all equipment and able to dive in all conditions. The teams can then hone those divers' skills in tactical operations, mine clearance, EOD, underwater ship repair and whatever else. 'All that Gucci stuff', wherever in the world it takes place, reinforces the original message: the bulk of the heavy lifting is done, and will always be done, right here at home. That's why there is a high failure rate in EOD, for instance: if you do not make the mark, you will not be waved through. For the students, passing that course is their licence to go overseas, if that is what they are aiming for. Not all divers are.

Being strapped into a bomb suit under the Afghan sun and walking down range to deal with an IED is not to everyone's taste. And not every diver wants to join TAG and shoot thousands of rounds a week and zoom about in special performance vehicles and choppers. In fact, one of the most popular jobs in the branch is underwater battle damage repairs. This is a corner of the branch where there is always a steady flow of challenging work to do. Kitted up in a hard-hat, surface-fed suit, they can be on projects that last weeks, such as changing a ship's propeller. On the rare occasion, they too get called upon to do what they are trained to do during war: help battle-damaged ships make it back to port. In July 2002, when HMS *Nottingham* hit Wolf Rock off Lord Howe Island, clearance divers carried out the emergency hull repairs that kept the stricken ship from sinking.

Darcey is keenly aware of *Penguin*'s history, if only because he's lived most of it. He joined not too long after the divers made their home here back in 1968. They took over a space that had been occupied by the Royal Navy 4th Submarine Squadron. An advance party was sent to reconnoitre the site and decide where to put what. They got distracted when they noticed that all the downpipes and guttering of their new abode were made of brass and copper. In no time they had stripped the place clean, sawed all the fittings into small pieces and flogged them for scrap metal for their Christmas party money.

The remainder of the team arrived straight from a job up at Nelson Bay. They approached *Penguin* aboard the dive tender HMAS *Turtle*, a converted bomb scow that had been used by the air force to arm seaplanes with depth charges and mines. As they neared the wharf an almighty racket erupted. The advance party was on the wharf lighting thunder flashes – small explosives thrown into the water to call divers to the surface – and dropping them into the hollow handles of their cylinder pump. When they followed one lit charge with another after three seconds, the first explosion would shoot the second charge out like a mortar. This was an auspicious occasion deserving of an improvised twenty-one-gun salute. Standing on the wharf, the commanding officer of *Penguin* must have wondered whether he could shunt these fast-and-loose newcomers off elsewhere. But it was too late – the divers had arrived.

Soon enough they were into their morning routine, doing their exercises, or 'physical jerks' as they called them, on the wharf before hitting the water. They would duck-dive nine metres without fins to grab mud off the bottom, then swim over to Balmoral, leopard-crawl along the beach, run up Awaba Street, through Mosman and back down to the base's front gate. There might be tip footy if they could make up the numbers with sailors attending the seamanship school. The physical demands have hardly changed. And the rigours of PT is what hooked Darcey from the start.

Even at fifty-two he has that classic diver's physique, so lean and chesty as to be almost conical. You could cork dams with these guys. Darcey may man a desk at *Penguin*, but he will never allow his body fat percentage to see double digits. He considers getting run into the ground every morning to be one of the perks of the job. Being able to hold his own with the younger men is a personal pride thing – physical excellence is the staple of his profession.

The way he sees it, he has no business doing anything but lead by example at the 'centre for excellence', as he calls the diving school. He wants his instructing staff to do the same, to take pride leading the navy's best: they are the men those wide-eyed kids who turn up for CDAT aspire to become. Darcey couldn't say that to a chief or an able seaman or anyone in between if he sat behind a desk with a big roll of flab hanging over his belt. Everything about Darcey says, 'Follow me, boys.' He makes damn sure of it.

Something else he is confident of is the continued relevance of the clearance diver. The Americans have been using dolphins and sea lions to do a range of activities better than divers – locating mines, retrieving objects dropped overboard, detecting enemy swimmers. They have also invested a lot of time and money refining their remote-control vehicle. Some people extrapolate from these developments and foresee the end of the clearance diver. This is rather unlikely.

For a start, UUVs are highly technical pieces of equipment. They break and they break down. Also, they cannot operate in rough seas – a pretty common condition off shallow beaches. Fixed with cameras, they are great for object identification, but a key problem is that they can't stop running into things. Let one loose in a shallow-water seabed littered with tall crops of coral and what you'll have is an expensive game of pinball.

'UUVs are great,' Darcey said, 'but if you're "red cell" [an opposing force], all you've got to do to secure a beach is lay a fishing net across the front of it and that's the end of your UUV. If it runs into that, it's ratshit.'

As for divers being replaced by mammals, they are a resource that only a superpower navy can afford. True, dolphins cannot be beaten for sonar acuity, but there will always be a need to deal with an underwater mine – not just find it and blow it up. You might have to exploit the mine for intelligence purposes, or maybe you'll risk taking the Opera House with it if you countermine in situ. A clearance diver can approach even the most sensitive mine and neutralise its sensor package without even laying a finger on it.

'You will never get the diver out of the water,' says Darcey.

And the same goes for land. Due to the demands of American IED teams in Iraq, advances in robotics have gone through the roof. An operator can inspect an IED remotely; he can take an X-ray; he can dig for wires; hook a string onto elements and yank them away from a safe distance. Yet, while there are now portable 'packbots' that are basically a remote camera platform and manipulator arm, it's not yet possible for them to deal with IEDs that are off the beaten track, elevated or on very rough terrain. Ultimately, the robot will remain a tool for the operator as opposed to his substitute.

Three or four years down the track the navy expects to have two new amphibious helicopter carriers, HMAS *Canberra* and HMAS *Adelaide*, on line. These vessels will be able to deliver land, sea and air assets anywhere in the world without need of a port, and there is certainly room on board for the clearance divers. Space has been allocated for all their gear – containers full of equipment, boats, UUVs, over-the-horizon insertion craft, swimmer-delivery vehicles. Darcey is excited for the divers of the future, and not just for professional reasons.

Pinned to a board overlooking his desk is a photo of a young sailor. His name is Jared: Darcey's nineteen-year-old son, who is currently doing his basic training course to become a clearance diver. There have been many sons who have followed their fathers, and even their grandfathers, into the branch, but rarely have both father and son served at the same time. Darcey knew Jared wanted to be a diver, and he was very proud when his son passed the CDAT. Then again, it was hardly surprising. He knew his son, how fit he was and how he had his mind set on becoming a diver. But every now and again the reality hits home: just a stone's throw away, down on the waterfront, Jared is learning to become a clearance diver.

'I have to check myself sometimes when I see him out there falling into his class. *Shit, that's my boy,*' said Darcey. More is left unsaid, but its essence is clearly felt to the heart.

'I guess it will hit home in August when he graduates and, you know . . .' At this point Darcey paused, leant to one side, pulled open a filing cabinet drawer and held up a piece of black cloth. 'And he gets one of these on his shoulder. You know, that will be quite emotional.'

BIBLIOGRAPHY

BOOKS

Blue, Lieutenant Commander Ross. *United and Undaunted*, The Naval Historical Society of Australia (Garden Island, NSW, 1976)

Cashford, Lieutenant Noel. *All Theirs!* ALD Design & Print (Sheffield, UK)

Churchill, Winston S. *The Second World War, Volume I: The Gathering Storm*, Houghton Mifflin Company (New York, 1948)

Fairfax, Dennis. *Royal Australian Navy in Vietnam*, Australian Government Publishing Service (Canberra, 1980)

Grosvenor, J. & Bates, L. M. *Open the Ports*, William Kimber & Co Ltd (London, 1956)

McAulay, Lex. *In the Ocean's Dark Embrace*, Banner Books (Maryborough, Qld, 1997)

Perryman, John & Mitchell, Brett. *Australia's Navy in Vietnam*, Topmill P/L (Silverwater, NSW)

Southall, Ivan. *Softly Tread the Brave*, Angus & Robertson (Australia, 1961)

Turner, John Frayn. *Fight For the Sea*. Naval Institute Press (Annapolis, MD, 2001)

WEBSITES

RAN Clearance Divers Association: rancd-association.com

Australian War Memorial: awm.gov.au

Royal Navy Minewarfare & Clearance Diving Officer's Association: mcdoa.org.uk

Imperial War Museum: iwm.org.uk

BBC: bbc.co.uk

World War II Today: ww2today.com

MAGAZINES

Australian & NZ Defender

OTHER

Mould, Commander John Stuart. Manuscript MSS1744, Australian War Memorial

Syme, Lieutenant Commander Hugh Randall. Audio: radio interview on 3TR '50 and Over', S00611, 14 July 1957, Australian War Memorial

ACKNOWLEDGEMENTS

I AM VERY grateful for the cooperation I received from the clearance diving community. It wasn't just about giving me the time of day or passing on someone's contact details – I was afforded a great deal of trust. Without it this book would be short on substance and bereft of intimacy. I would single out a few gentlemen who went the extra yard, but I think they would prefer me not to. Stuff it: thanks to Jake Linton, Larry Digney, Tony Ey, Eric McKenzie and Chris White. But whatever broad support existed, the author's responsibilities are not shared. Any mistakes on the page are my fault alone.

I met and spoke with divers of all ages and every era. Their personalities differed but they did share a few traits. A natural, ingrained expertise shone through whenever they spoke about diving. There was the comfortably worn discipline, the

281

hearty ego and the sense of being a bit privileged and a great deal proud. In the end it does not matter who has been cited in this book and who has not. If the essence of the clearance diver can be grasped, then it is every diver's story.

I owe thanks to many people outside the diving fraternity. For one, there is Ivan Southall. His terrific book *Softly Tread the Brave* brought to life the deeds of John Stuart Mould and Hugh Randall Syme. Without Southall the wider memory of two of Australia's most decorated servicemen would have survived in the most perfunctory of forms, so easily undervalued.

Many thanks to Lieutenant Kate Mathews and Commander Adrian Kemp for bringing the Royal Australian Navy to the table on this project. With the able assistance of Lieutenant Ben Willee, Commander Kemp cleared the way for my extraordinary access to the world of navy divers. I also would like to thank John Pennefather, scientist officer at the RAN Submarine and Underwater Medicine Unit, HMAS *Penguin*. Not just a font of information, he was a valuable sounding board.

If it were not for Nikki Christer and Alison Urquhart at Random House, I would have played no role in this project. They entrusted me to tell this story, and I am glad they did. Thanks to my agent, Jane Burridge, who always had my back, and to Brandon VanOver, Random House's managing editor, who covered front and side.

And to Celia: I hate to think where my heart and head would be without you.

INDEX

Photo: Tim Thatcher

GREGOR SALMON IS a Sydney-based writer. He is the author of *Poppy*, an account of his first-hand investigation into Afghanistan's opium trade, and *Heart Soul Fire*, which he wrote with boxer Paul Briggs. Over the years he has written, edited and produced his way through a host of magazines, television shows and internet sites.